READING/WRITING
COMPANION

Mc
Graw
Hill

COVER: James Haskins

mheducation.com/prek-12

Send all inquiries to:
McGraw-Hill Education
Two Penn Plaza
New York, New York 10121

ISBN: 978-0-07-700542-9
MHID: 0-07-700542-2

Printed in the United States of America.

9 LMN 24 23   B

Welcome to Wonders !

Read exciting **Literature**, **Science**, and **Social Studies** texts!

★ **LEARN** about the world around you!

★ **THINK**, **SPEAK**, and **WRITE** about genres!

★ **COLLABORATE** in discussion and inquiry!

★ **EXPRESS** yourself!

my.mheducation.com
Use your student login to read core texts, practice grammar and spelling, explore research projects and more!

UNIT 5

GENRE STUDY 1 **EXPOSITORY TEXT**

GENRE STUDY 2 **HISTORICAL FICTION**

Dennis Crawford/Alamy Stock Photo

GENRE STUDY **3 ARGUMENTATIVE TEXT**

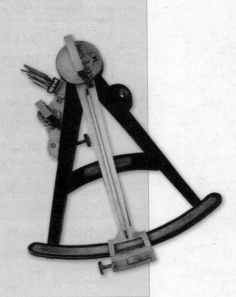

WRAP UP THE UNIT

 Digital Tools Find this eBook and other resources at **my.mheducation.com**

GENRE STUDY 1 **EXPOSITORY TEXT**

GENRE STUDY 2 **EXPOSITORY TEXT**

GENRE STUDY 3 POETRY

WRAP UP THE UNIT

 Digital Tools Find this eBook and other resources at **my.mheducation.com**

Talk About It

Essential Question

How do people benefit from innovation?

The sleek and aerodynamic train in this photo runs on the Beijing–Shanghai High-Speed Railway. It travels between the two Chinese cities at speeds between 155 and 185 miles per hour. On older trains, traveling between Beijing and Shanghai took ten hours or more. Now, the trip takes less than five hours. This is just one example of an innovative modification that has made people's lives easier.

Look at the photograph. Talk to a partner about what you see, and compare the train to trains you are familiar with. Discuss what you know about positive effects of innovation. Write your ideas in the web.

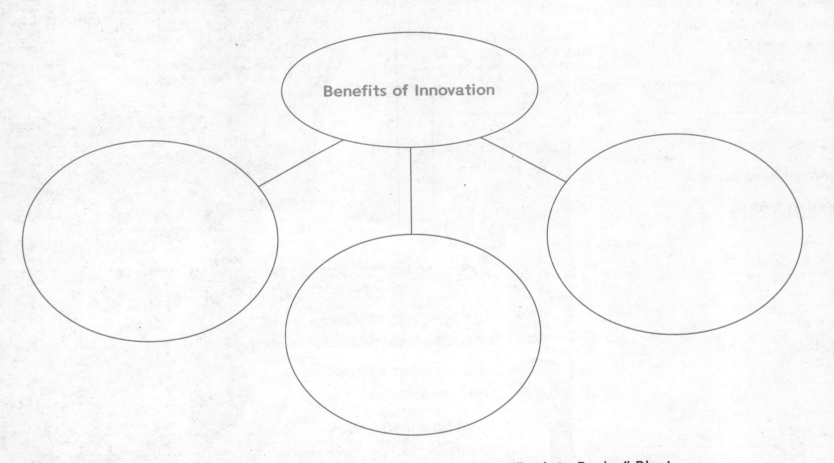

Benefits of Innovation

BLAST BACK! studysync

Go online to **my.mheducation.com** and read the "Back to Basics" Blast. Think about the effects of innovations in how we grow our food. Then blast back your response.

TAKE NOTES

Asking questions before you begin reading a text can help you set a purpose by identifying what you hope to learn. Preview the headings, photographs, and other text features. Then write a question you have below. Look for the answer as you read.

_____

_____

_____

As you read, take note of

Interesting Words _____

_____

_____

Key Details _____

_____

_____

_____

_____

The Science of Silk

(t)De Agostini Picture Library/De Agostini/Getty Images;
(tr)Frank Greenaway/Dorling Kindersley/Getty Images;
(c)Gio Barto/Photographer's Choice/Getty Images;
(b)Dennis Crawford/Alamy Stock Photo

Essential Question

How do people benefit from innovation?

Read how innovations in silk production have made this once rare cloth available to many people.

When the silk-making process was first developed five thousand years ago in China, silk was a rare and expensive luxury. Silk would still be **sparse** today if people had not engaged in the **manipulation** of a natural process. Sericulture, the breeding of silkworms to produce silk, has improved greatly over the centuries. The technologies used in making silk thread and weaving silk fabric have also benefited from important innovations.

A Better Silkworm

The silkworm is the larva, or caterpillar, of *Bombyx mori,* the domesticated silk moth typically used in silk production. (The name *Bombyx mori* means "mulberry silk moth.") This animal's life cycle has four stages: egg; larva that makes the cocoon; pupa that changes inside the cocoon; and winged adult moth. Silk is the material that the larva naturally produces to make its cocoon.

Bombyx mori is a hybrid, the result of breeding particular species over many years. This selective **modification** of inherited traits was done to make a stronger and more productive moth. For example, a *Bombyx mori* moth lays about 500 eggs, more than other species. The eggs are hardier than other silkworm eggs. As a result, more of them survive to develop into larvae. The larvae are also healthy. They eat enough to increase 10,000 times in size in just four to six weeks.

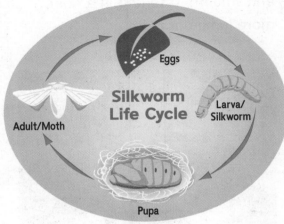

Silkworm Life Cycle

Eggs

Larva/ Silkworm

Pupa

Adult/Moth

Most moths fly during their adult stage to find mates and places with plentiful food to lay their eggs. But *Bombyx mori* is a **mutated** species of moth that is unable to fly. For this reason, it relies entirely on humans to provide its larvae with a special diet of **nutrients** from the leaves of white mulberry trees. Humans must also ensure that the eggs are kept at a temperature of 65° to 77° F until they hatch.

FIND TEXT EVIDENCE

Read

Paragraphs 1–2
Reread

Underline text evidence that tells how the *Bombyx mori* moth creates silk.

Paragraphs 3–4
Cause and Effect

Why do more *Bombyx mori* eggs develop into larvae than do the eggs of other silk moth species?

_____

_____

Diagram

Look at the diagram. **Circle** the text on this page that it illustrates.

Reread
Author's Craft

Why do you think the author chose to include a diagram on this page?

SHARED READ

FIND TEXT EVIDENCE

Read

Paragraph 1

Cause and Effect

Circle the signal word that helps you identify the effect the round, smooth *Bombyx mori* filament has on silk. **Underline** the effect.

Paragraphs 2–4

Reread

Why was silk production once an inefficient process?

_____

_____

_____

_____

Draw a box around text that describes one method people developed to speed up the process.

Reread

Author's Craft

Why is "From Cocoon to Thread" a good heading for this section?

People go through this great effort because the silk of *Bombyx mori* is strong and breaks less often than "wild" silk. The filament from a single cocoon can be 3,000 feet long when it is unwound. *Bombyx mori* silk is whiter than wild silk, so it can absorb more dye. The filament is also round and smooth, resulting in a finer, more luminous cloth.

Silkworm spinning its cocoon (top); Weaving silk fabric in Myanmar

From Cocoon to Thread

For thousands of years, raising silkworms to make silk was an important part of Chinese culture. Women and girls were responsible for tending the worms, processing the cocoons, spinning the thread, and weaving fabric by hand. These painstaking chores produced beautiful results. They were also **inefficient**, consuming many hours per day and producing only a small amount of silk cloth.

Much of the ancient process survives in current practices. Cocoons are still harvested about eight or nine days after they form. They are placed in water so that they soften enough to be unwound without breaking the filament of raw silk. To avoid building up a **surplus** of unusable cocoons, a time-saving technique called *reeling* has been developed to unwind several cocoons at once. The cocoons are gently brushed to find the loose ends. Then the filaments are wound onto a reel.

A single raw silk filament is too thin to use for weaving. So the next common step in the process, called *throwing,* involves twisting several filaments together to form a thread. The thrown threads are then wound onto small spools called bobbins.

A secret for 3,000 years, Chinese sericulture spread to Korea about 200 B.C. , and to India, Japan, and Persia about 300 A.D.

Advances in Silk Technology

Silk moth eggs and the closely guarded secret of sericulture had to be smuggled out of China before other countries could make silk. Once the basic process was known, people sought to improve the technologies used in making silk filaments into cloth. One important invention was the French reeling machine. Its great innovation was to speed up the reeling process and reduce waste.

About 1800, the invention of the Jacquard loom enabled silk weavers to create complex designs quickly. This mechanized loom required strong threads, so even better sericulture practices were developed. More recently, **industrial** weaving machines began using air to push the thread rapidly back and forth. This meant that fewer workers were needed to oversee the looms and that costs could be lowered. As a result, fine silk products were soon available at prices that more people could afford.

Today, China remains the leading producer of silk. But the demand for fine mulberry silk products reaches far beyond China's borders. For this reason, people will continue seeking better, more economical ways to produce silk.

Summarize

Use your notes to orally summarize the process of silk production, including silk's creation and later use in fabrics.

FIND TEXT EVIDENCE

Read

Paragraph 1
Context Clues

Circle the context clue that helps you know what *smuggled* means. Write the meaning here.

_____

Paragraphs 2–3
Cause and Effect

Underline the cause of more affordable silk products.

Map

What additional information about the spread of sericulture do the map and caption provide?

_____

_____

Reread

Author's Craft

How does the author organize the text to help you understand the effect of smuggling the secret of sericulture out of China?

Vocabulary

Use the example sentences to talk with a partner about each word. Then answer the questions.

industrial

I live in an **industrial** area with many automobile factories.

How is an industrial area different from farmland?

_____

_____

inefficient

It is **inefficient** to eat soup with a fork.

What is another inefficient thing to do?

_____

_____

manipulation

Special computer software allows for the **manipulation** of photographs.

How are the meanings of *manipulation* and *change* related?

_____

_____

modification

The tailor's **modification** to the sleeve made the shirt fit perfectly.

What is a synonym for *modification*?

_____

_____

mutated

The scientist learned that the new virus was a **mutated** form of the virus that causes the flu.

What is an antonym of *mutated*?

_____

_____

Build Your Word List Reread the first paragraph on page 3. Circle the word *process*. In your writer's notebook, use a word web to write more forms of the word, such as *processors*. Use a dictionary to help you find more related words.

nutrients

Eating foods with vitamins and other **nutrients** keeps our bodies healthy.

Name something you eat that contains important nutrients.

_____

_____

_____

sparse

Attendance at the football game was **sparse** due to the rainy weather.

What things are sparse in a desert?

_____

_____

_____

surplus

We have a **surplus** of food left over from the celebration.

Describe a time you had a surplus of something.

_____

_____

_____

Context Clues

When reading an expository text, you can use context clues to find or verify the meanings of unfamiliar or multiple-meaning words. Look for clues that show cause-and-effect relationships.

🔍 FIND TEXT EVIDENCE

I was unsure of the meaning of the word filament *on page 4 of "The Science of Silk." Context clues in the sentence indicate that the long filament is the result, or effect, of unwinding a single cocoon, so I think* filament *means "a very thin fiber."*

The <u>filament</u> from a single cocoon can be 3,000 feet long when it is unwound.

Your Turn Use context clues that indicate cause-and-effect relationships to find the meanings of the words below from "The Science of Silk."

hybrid, *page 3* _____

productive, *page 3* _____

oversee, *page 5* _____

Reread

Expository texts such as "The Science of Silk" may explain steps involved in a complex process. When reading about a complex or unfamiliar topic, reread portions of the text to make sure you understand the information.

🔍 FIND TEXT EVIDENCE

You may not have understood why people supply food for the *Bombyx mori* larvae. Reread "A Better Silkworm" on page 3 of "The Science of Silk."

Quick Tip

Taking notes or marking up the selection is helpful when rereading a text for a specific purpose. Underline, highlight, or post a sticky note in the margin when you find information that is important or will help you answer your question.

> Page 3
>
> Most moths fly during their adult stage to find mates and places with plentiful food to lay their eggs. But *Bombyx mori* is a **mutated** species of moth that is unable to fly. For this reason, it relies entirely on humans to provide its larvae with a special diet of **nutrients** from the leaves of white mulberry trees. Humans must also ensure that the eggs are kept at a temperature of 65° to 77° F until they hatch.

I read that "most moths fly" to find food for their larvae, but Bombyx mori *is "unable to fly." I can infer that silk moth larvae would not survive if humans did not supply food.*

Your Turn Reread "Advances in Silk Technology" on page 5. How have different inventions made silk production more efficient and affordable?

_____

_____

_____

_____

Maps and Diagrams

"The Science of Silk" is an example of an expository text. An expository text may include text features such as maps, diagrams, photographs, and captions. These text features support the information in a text or provide additional information that is relevant to the topic.

FIND TEXT EVIDENCE

I can tell "The Science of Silk" is an expository text because it explains how people produced silk throughout history. It includes text features, such as a diagram that details a natural occurrence discussed in the text and a map that shows the locations of places described in the text.

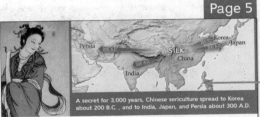

Page 5

A secret for 3,000 years, Chinese sericulture spread to Korea about 200 B.C., and to India, Japan, and Persia about 300 A.D.

Advances in Silk Technology

Silk moth eggs and the closely guarded secret of sericulture had to be smuggled out of China before other countries could make silk. Once the basic process was known, people sought to improve the technologies used in making silk filaments into cloth. One important invention was the French reeling machine. Its great innovation was to speed up the reeling process and reduce waste.

About 1800, the invention of the Jacquard loom enabled silk weavers to create complex designs quickly. This mechanized loom required strong threads, so even better sericulture practices were developed. More recently, **industrial** weaving machines

began using air to push the thread rapidly back and forth. This meant that fewer workers were needed to oversee the looms and that costs could be lowered. As a result, fine silk products were soon available at prices that more people could afford.

Today, China remains the leading producer of silk. But the demand for fine mulberry silk products reaches far beyond China's borders. For this reason, people will continue seeking better, more economical ways to produce silk.

Summarize

Use your notes to orally summarize the process of silk production, including silk's creation and later use in fabrics.

Diagrams

Diagrams illustrate concepts described in the text.

Maps

Maps can show a visual representation of ideas in the text that relate to geography.

COLLABORATE

Your Turn How is the information in the diagram on page 3 and map on page 5 helpful in understanding sericulture?

_____

_____

_____

_____

_____

Cause and Effect

An author may organize an expository text to show the cause-and-effect relationships among parts of a process. Explaining how various steps in a process achieve specific results helps readers understand why the process evolved the way it did.

🔍 FIND TEXT EVIDENCE

When I reread the section "A Better Silkworm" on pages 3–4 of "The Science of Silk," I can look for cause-and-effect signal words and phrases, such as because, so, *and* as a result, *to help me identify why people bred* Bombyx mori *for use in the silk production process.*

Quick Tip

Authors occasionally describe cause-and-effect relationships without using signal words. In this case, you can identify causes and effects by asking yourself: *What happened? Why did it happen?* The answer to *Why did it happen?* is the cause. The answer to *What happened?* is the effect.

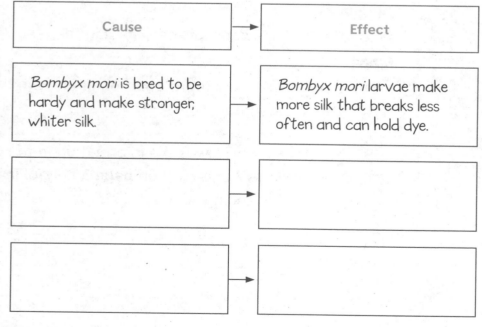

Cause	→	Effect
Bombyx mori is bred to be hardy and make stronger, whiter silk.	→	*Bombyx mori* larvae make more silk that breaks less often and can hold dye.
	→	
	→	

Your Turn Reread "The Science of Silk." Find cause-and-effect relationships and list them in your graphic organizer on page 11.

Cause	→	Effect
Bombyx mori is bred to be hardy and make stronger, whiter silk.	→	*Bombyx mori* larvae make more silk that breaks less often and can hold dye.
	→	
	→	
	→	

Respond to Reading

COLLABORATE

Discuss the prompt below. Think about how the author of "The Science of Silk" describes and presents the information. Use your notes and graphic organizer.

How does the author help you understand how people benefited from innovations in sericulture and silk production?

_____

_____

_____

_____

_____

_____

_____

_____

_____

_____

_____

_____

_____

_____

Identify and Gather Information

When you research a topic, you **identify and gather information** from a variety of sources. Use reliable, up-to-date sources with information relevant to your topic. Note your sources so you can cite them later. Do the following to help you identify and gather relevant information:

- Consider the reason for your research.
- List specific questions you have about the important ideas and write down the answers as you research.
- Create an outline that identifies the main ideas. Think about and look for additional information you might need to complete the outline and support your ideas.

How can you confirm that information from a source is helpful?

_____

_____

Create a Chart With a partner or group, create a chart that tracks the history of three different kinds of produce. This can include fruits, vegetables, and other plants used for food. In your chart, include answers to these questions:

- Where was the produce first used as a food source?
- What is an early mention in literature or history?
- What is one interesting fact about the food?

Record your sources in your chart. Add photos or other visuals that show what the produce you chose looks like. You will share your chart with your classmates.

Produce	Banana
Place of Origin	Southeast Asia
First Mentioned	Early Greek, Latin, and Arab sources
Fact	The banana plant can grow to be 20 feet tall.
Sources	www.encyclopedia.web www.tropicalplants.web

The chart above shows information that one group researched for an entry about bananas. What is another fact the group members might identify and include in their research?

_____

_____

_____

Before Columbus: The Americas of 1491

Literature Anthology: pages 332–343

? How does the author use photographs to help you understand more about maize?

Talk About It Look at the photograph on **Literature Anthology** page 334 and caption on page 335. Talk with a partner about what the image shows and how it helps you understand the selection.

Cite Text Evidence What details in the image tell you more about maize? Write clues in the chart and tell how they help you understand maize.

Quick Tip

When studying details in a photograph, be sure to look for and read any caption that goes with it. Captions tell you more about what the photograph shows. They often provide information that you won't find in the main text of the selection.

Clues	How They Help

Write The author uses photographs to _____

_____

_____

What is the author's point of view about the invention of the *milpa*?

 Talk About It Reread the first two paragraphs on **Literature Anthology** page 340. Talk with a partner about what the *milpa* is.

Cite Text Evidence What text evidence shows how the author feels about the invention of the *milpa*? Write it in the chart.

Text Evidence
Text Evidence
Text Evidence
Author's Point of View

Write The author's point of view about the invention of the *milpa* is _____

_____

_____

_____

 Make Inferences

According to the author, one effect of adding fertilizer to soil is that it may unbalance the ecosystem by causing "excess growth" of algae in bodies of water. What can you infer about algae from this information? How does it affect the author's point of view about the *milpa*?

? **How does the author use the map to help you understand maize and its impact on Mesoamerica?**

Talk About It Reread **Literature Anthology** page 342 and analyze the map on page 343. Talk with a partner about Mesoamerica and how the map supports the text.

Cite Text Evidence How does the map help clarify the text? Write text evidence in the chart.

Evidence from the Map	How It Clarifies Text

Write The author uses the map to help me understand _____

_____

_____

Evaluate Information

On Literature Anthology page 342, the author says that the development of maize as a crop "was part of a great explosion of creativity that took place in Mesoamerica at that time." What might be the reason for this? How might creativity and agricultural development be dependent on each other?

Respond to Reading

Discuss the prompt below. Consider how the author conveys information about the development and importance of maize. Use your notes and graphic organizer.

How does Charles C. Mann use text features and the organization of this selection to help you understand how people benefited from the innovation of maize?

_____

_____

_____

_____

_____

_____

_____

_____

_____

_____

_____

_____

_____

Quick Tip

Use these sentence starters to talk about and cite text evidence.

Charles C. Mann uses photographs, sidebars, and maps to . . .

He shares his point of view to help me . . .

I see how people benefited from the innovation of maize because . . .

Self-Selected Reading

Choose a text and fill in your writer's notebook with the title, author, and genre of the book. Record your purpose for reading. For example, you may be reading to answer a question or for entertainment.

Looking Back to Move Forward

Literature Anthology:
pages 346–349

Ancient Cures

1   Over two decades ago, two divers plunged into the murky depths of the Mediterranean Sea off the coast of Italy. Their mission was the exploration of a 50-foot long shipwreck. It had been lost beneath the waves over 2,000 years ago. As they trained their underwater lights across the vast hulk, they spotted amphorae—vases used for holding olive oil and other products. But a close inspection revealed something much more remarkable. Pulled from the wreck, the explorers found tin-lined wooden containers. They held tablets the size of small coins.

2   Scientists later found that these tablets were probably pills that the ship's sailors would have swallowed with water, perhaps when they felt seasick. This sort of medicine is nothing new to us today. At the time, however, they must have been something new, for they may be the oldest pills discovered.

Reread the two introductory paragraphs from "Looking Back to Move Forward." **Circle** the sentences from paragraph 1 that tell what the explorers discovered. **Underline** the sentence in paragraph 2 that tells why this discovery is important.

COLLABORATE

Talk with a partner about the discovery and its importance. How do you think this discovery could affect science today?

_____

_____

_____

1   Researchers also continue to look at the past in order to investigate cures that were used long ago. One such opportunity presented itself with the discovery of that ancient Roman shipwreck in the Mediterranean. Although the pills were discovered in 1989, recent advances in DNA research are now making it possible to better understand what chemical compounds these pills contained. This research will also help determine what illnesses the pills were used to treat. The hope is that advances in technology will build upon ancient wisdom.

Reread paragraph 1, the concluding paragraph in "Looking Back to Move Forward." **Underline** the sentences that tell how researchers today use such discoveries as the tablets from the shipwreck. Explain how they do so in your own words.

_____

_____

_____

_____

COLLABORATE

Talk with a partner about why ancient medicines are of interest to researchers. How can we benefit from the knowledge they gain about these substances?

_____

_____

_____

_____

? **Why is "Looking Back to Move Forward" a good title for this selection?**

Talk About It Reread the excerpts on pages 18–19. Talk with a partner about the message the author wants the reader to understand.

Cite Text Evidence Record text evidence from each of the excerpted paragraphs that helps to communicate the author's message. Explain the author's purpose for the way in which he or she concludes the passage.

Quick Tip

To understand the author's purpose for the way in which he or she concludes the text, compare the conclusion on page 19 to the two paragraphs from the introduction to the text on page 18. What information or ideas does the author repeat or build on in the conclusion?

Details

↓

Author's Purpose

Write "Looking Back to Move Forward" is a good title because _____

_____

_____

_____

Charles Stirling (Diving)/Alamy Stock Photo

Text Features

Authors of expository texts often use text features, such as diagrams, to support and expand upon important points made in the main text. Diagrams are especially useful for showing steps in a process or describing the way something works.

FIND TEXT EVIDENCE

In "Looking Back to Move Forward" on **Literature Anthology** page 348, the author includes a kind of diagram called a flowchart to show the steps in making medicine from the quinine tree.

Your Turn Reread "Today's Medicines" on Literature Anthology pages 347–348. Then analyze the flowchart on page 348.

- How does the flowchart add to your understanding of the main text?

_____

_____

_____

_____

- How does the author use visuals to help you understand the content of the flowchart? _____

_____

_____

_____

To determine which text feature is best to use, an author thinks about his or her purpose. When including text features in your own writing, ask yourself: *What do I want my readers to know? What kind of text feature will help them understand the ideas I want to communicate?*

Text Connections

? **How is pre-European innovation made apparent by this aerial photograph, the investigation into the origin of maize in *Before Columbus: The Americas of 1491*, and the discovery of medicine in an ancient Roman shipwreck in "Looking Back to Move Forward"?**

COLLABORATE

Talk About It Look at the photograph and read the caption. Talk with a partner about the location of the buildings, their size, and the technology required to create such an elaborate site.

Cite Text Evidence **Circle** clues in the photograph that show the advanced knowledge of building that was needed to construct Machu Picchu. **Underline** evidence in the caption that tells when it was built. Think about the selections you read this week. Talk about how important innovation is and how people benefit from it.

Write I understand how important innovation is

because _____

_____

_____

_____

_____

_____

_____

Quick Tip

As you study the photograph, consider when Machu Picchu was built. Think about how builders living hundreds of years ago were able to create the structure without the modern construction equipment builders use today.

This photograph presents an aerial view of the Machu Picchu site in the Cusco Region of Peru. This grand group of structures was built before the Spanish Conquest in the mid-1400s by the Incan civilization.

Rodrigo Torres/Glow Images

Present Your Work

COLLABORATE

Discuss how you will present your chart and visuals displaying the history of three different kinds of produce. Use the Presenting Checklist as you practice your presentation. Discuss the sentence starters below and write your answers.

One unexpected fact I learned was _____

_____

_____

I am curious to find out more about _____

_____

_____

Quick Tip

Displaying content in a variety of colors will make your chart more visually appealing and easier for your audience to see. If needed, consider making copies for classmates or using presentation software to display the chart.

✓ Presenting Checklist

- ☐ Define each person's role in the presentation and rehearse the presentation in advance.
- ☐ Make sure your ideas are logically organized.
- ☐ Make appropriate eye contact with the audience.
- ☐ Speak loudly and clearly.
- ☐ Respond politely and concisely to questions from the audience.

Africa Studio/Shutterstock

Literature Anthology: pages 332–343

Expert Model

Features of a Research Report

A research report is a type of expository text. It draws on a variety of sources to provide information about a topic. A research report

- has a clear central topic;

- develops the topic with facts, details, quotations, and other information gathered from reliable sources;

- uses transition words and phrases to clarify relationships between ideas.

Word Wise

On page 335, notice the descriptions the author uses, such as "the narrow 'waist' of southern Mexico" and "This jumble of mountains." The vivid descriptive language helps readers understand the geography of the area and draws them into reading about the topic.

Analyze an Expert Model Studying expository texts will help you plan and write a research report. **Reread** the paragraph on page 333 and the first two paragraphs on page 335 of *Before Columbus: The Americas of 1491* in the **Literature Anthology**. Then answer the questions below.

What do you think will be the central topic of this chapter from *Before Columbus: The Americas of 1491?* _____

_____

What facts, details, or other information help you know what the central

topic is? _____

_____

_____

_____

Plan: Choose Your Topic

Brainstorm With a partner, talk about historical civilizations that you know of, such as ancient Egypt or the Inca Empire. There are many historical civilizations. Ask your teacher for additional ideas. As you choose a civilization, think about the achievements or innovations the civilization is known for. You can refer to print or online encyclopedias for help. Write your ideas on a separate sheet of paper.

Writing Prompt Choose one historical civilization from your list. Write a research report in which you describe and explain the significance of one of the innovations or achievements the civilization is known for.

I will research and write a report about _____

_____ .

Purpose and Audience Who will read your research report? Will you write to inform, persuade, or entertain this audience? Think about the language you will use. Will it be formal or informal? Why?

My purpose for writing is to _____

My audience will be _____

I will use _____ language to write my research report.

Plan In your writer's notebook, make a Main Idea and Details chart to plan your research report. Fill in the Main Idea box with a statement that describes the main idea of your research report.

Quick Tip

As you brainstorm ideas, think about questions you have about the historical group and its innovation or achievement. Add them to your notes. Use these questions to guide your research. Look for answers to these questions as you read your sources.

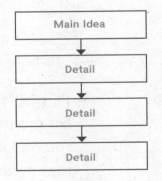

Main Idea

Detail

Detail

Detail

Plan: Research

Choose and Evaluate Sources As you research your topic, make sure your sources are accurate and current. Choose reliable sources, such as encyclopedias, books, periodicals, and websites that end in *.gov* or *.edu*. To check that your sources are reliable, answer these questions:

- Who wrote this source, and is the author reputable?

- When was this source published, and is the information current?

- Can I confirm the information in this source with a second source?

List two sources that you will use to find information for your report.

1 _____

2 _____

Take Notes As you research, add details to your Main Idea and Details chart. Keep track of sources by recording the author, title, and publication information in your notes. This will help you prepare a works cited page, or list of sources used in your research. A works cited entry for an online article might read:

"Roman Aqueducts." *Ancient History*. www.ancienthistory.web/
    roman_aqueducts. Accessed May 4 2018.

Digital Tools

For more information on how to effectively review sources you find as you research, watch "Skim and Scan." Go to **my.mheducation.com**.

Draft

Supporting Details Authors of research reports use relevant facts, statistics, quotations, examples, and other details to support their ideas. In the excerpt from "The Science of Silk" below, facts about *Bombyx mori* and a concrete measurement help the author explain why silk created from this hybrid moth is superior to other silks.

> People go through this great effort because the silk of *Bombyx mori* is strong and breaks less often than "wild" silk. The filament from a single cocoon can be 3,000 feet long when it is unwound. *Bombyx mori* silk is whiter than wild silk, so it can absorb more dye.

Now use the paragraph as a model to write about an important idea you will include in your report. Support the idea with details from your research.

_____

_____

_____

_____

_____

 Write a Draft Use your Main Idea and Details graphic organizer to help write your draft in your writer's notebook. Avoid plagiarizing by paraphrasing and properly citing your sources of information.

Grammar Connections

Make sure you correctly format the titles of the sources you cite. Titles of long works, such as books and documentary films, should be italicized or underlined. Titles of articles and websites should be set in quotation marks. For example:

- "The Science of Silk"
- *Before Columbus: The Americas of 1491*

Revise

Transitions Effective writers include transition words and phrases to present ideas clearly and help readers understand the connections between ideas. Examples of transition words and phrases include *however, although, in addition, yet,* and *as a result*. Read the sample paragraph below. Then revise it, making sure to add transition words and phrases that clarify how ideas are related.

> The Aztec were a Mesoamerican culture. They made chocolate. Their chocolate was not like most of today's chocolate. It was made from the beans of the cacao tree. So is today's chocolate. Today's chocolate usually has sugar and is sweet. The Aztec chocolate did not have sugar and was bitter. The Aztec called it *xocoatl*. This name meant "food of the gods."

_____

_____

_____

_____

Revision As you revise your draft, make sure you've included relevant details that clearly support your topic and are based in research. Add appropriate transition words and phrases to show how ideas are related.

Peer Conferences

Review a Draft Listen carefully as a partner reads his or her work aloud. Take notes about what you liked and what was difficult to follow. Begin by telling what you liked about the draft. Ask questions that will help the writer think more about the writing. Make suggestions that you think will make the writing stronger. Use these sentence starters:

I enjoyed this part of your draft because . . .

Your research would be more credible if you . . .

Can you explain how this detail supports the idea that . . .

Connecting these ideas with a transition word, phrase, or sentence would help . . .

Partner Feedback After your partner gives you feedback on your draft, write one of the suggestions that you will use in your revision. Refer to the rubric on page 31 as you give feedback.

Based on my partner's feedback, I will _____

_____

_____

_____

After you finish giving each other feedback, reflect on the peer conference. What was helpful? What might you do differently next time?

Revision As you revise your draft, use the Revising Checklist to help you figure out what text you may need to move, elaborate on, or delete. Remember to use the rubric on page 31 to help you with your revision.

✔ Revising Checklist

☐ Do I consistently use language appropriate for my topic and audience?

☐ Is information from my research relevant to my topic and from credible sources?

☐ Do I need to add more facts, statistics, examples, or other details and evidence to support my main ideas?

☐ Have I used transitions to effectively show the relationships between ideas?

Edit and Proofread

When you **edit** and **proofread** your writing, you look for and correct mistakes in spelling, punctuation, capitalization, and grammar. Reading through a revised draft multiple times can help you make sure you're correcting any errors. Use the checklist below to edit your sentences.

Tech Tip

Spell checkers don't always flag homophones used incorrectly. Often, a homophone is spelled correctly, but it's the wrong word for the sentence. For example: *Researchers consulted they're maps.* The word *they're* should be *their*. Make a list of common homophones. Look for them specifically as you edit and proofread.

Editing Checklist

☐ Are all introductory transition words and phrases followed by a comma?

☐ Are there any run-on sentences or sentence fragments?

☐ Are all homophones used and spelled correctly?

☐ Are all proper nouns and adjectives capitalized?

☐ Are cited titles correctly formatted with italics, underlining, or quotation marks?

☐ Are all words spelled correctly?

List two mistakes you found as you proofread your research report.

1 _____

_____

2 _____

_____

Publish, Present, and Evaluate

Publishing When you **publish** your writing, you create a clean, neat final copy free of mistakes. As you write, be sure to print neatly. Consider adding visuals such as a timeline, maps, or illustrations to help readers better understand the information in your research report.

Presentation When you are ready to **present** your work, rehearse your presentation. Use the Presenting Checklist to help you.

Evaluate After you publish your writing, use the rubric below to **evaluate** your writing.

What did you do successfully? _____

What needs more work? _____

_____

4	3	2	1
• has a clear central topic • supports the central topic with many details gathered from reliable sources • uses a variety of transition words and phrases to clarify relationships among ideas	• has a central topic that is mostly clear • supports the central idea with some details from reliable sources • uses some transition words and phrases to clarify relationships among ideas	• makes an effort to inform readers but the central topic is unclear • includes a few supporting details gathered only from a few sources • uses a few transition words and phrases to clarify relationships among ideas	• has no central topic and does not inform readers • does not include any supporting details • does not use transition words or phrases to clarify relationships among ideas

Talk About It

Essential Question

How do people show inner strength?

In this photo, a student is preparing for her piano recital. She has been practicing for weeks, but is still nervous about performing. She plans to draw on her inner strength when she plays. Her teacher has told her that he believes she has the fortitude to give a great performance. Whatever happens, she knows it will be up to her once she begins to play.

What does the phrase "inner strength" mean to you? Have you had times when you needed inner strength to accomplish something? Discuss what you know about ways people draw on inner strength. Write your ideas in the web.

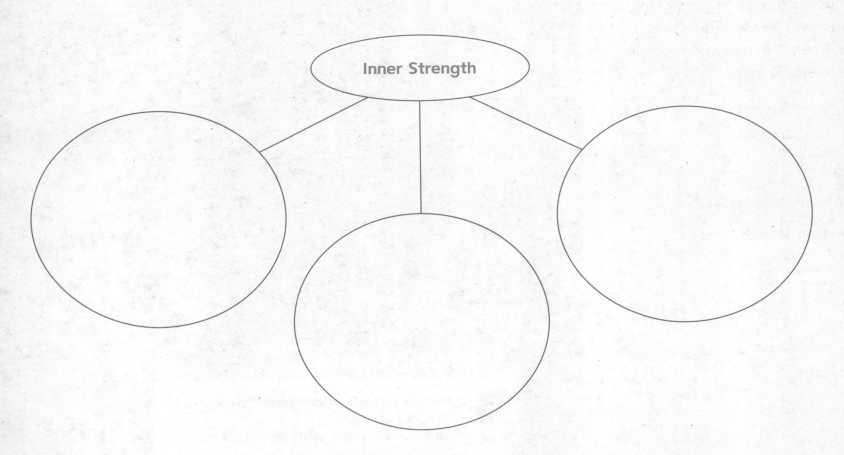

Inner Strength

Go online to **my.mheducation.com** and read the "Pathfinder" Blast. Think about what sort of situations require inner strength. What are some ways people show their inner strength? Then blast back your response.

TAKE NOTES

Asking questions about story elements, such as character, plot, or setting, and looking for answers as you read will help you focus on story information. Preview the title and illustrations. What questions do you have? Write a question below. Keep it in mind and look for answers as you read.

_____
_____
_____
_____

As you read, take note of

Interesting Words _____

_____
_____
_____

Key Details _____

_____
_____
_____

JOURNEY TO Freedom

Essential Question

? How do people show inner strength?

Read about a girl who discovers her inner strength when she is called upon to help people escaping slavery.

It is early summer 1851, and 12-year-old Abigail Parker is still finding her way after the death of her mother the previous winter. Her father has recently made their Massachusetts farm a station on the Underground Railroad, and the two nervously await their first "delivery" of people on their way to Canada to escape slavery.

I could not sit for being so fretful, so I paced and sometimes paused to peer out the window. Mother often said, "Patience is bitter, but its fruit is sweet." If only I were possessed of her calm.

"I see no sign of our four guests," Papa announced as he returned from checking outdoors, fueling my fears that they had met with misfortune. Just then, a sudden knock sounded, and my heart took to pounding as Papa opened the door to two weary women on the **stoop**. He assisted the older one, who appeared to be about 60, to a chair by the hearth. Her companion was maybe 14. Papa directed me to poke up the fire and fetch food and drink.

When the women got back their breath, Papa asked, "What of the others? Did they not accompany you?"

"Just Nellis and me," the girl declared, and the older woman presented a letter.

Papa handed the crumpled paper to me, saying, "If you would, Abby. My eyes fail me in dim light."

I brought the letter close by a candle and commenced reading:
"Dear Jonathan,
*I send you Nellis and Emma, separate from their two companions, who have fallen ill with fever, one seriously. We have insufficient room to hide four until they recover, so I hope you are **disposed** to shelter them until further transport can be arranged.*
Respectfully,
Jacob."

Papa nodded and said, "We must see to their safety and comfort." I guided them to the attic hiding place and wished them a peaceful night.

FIND TEXT EVIDENCE

Read

Introduction–Paragraph 1

Adages and Proverbs

An adage is a traditional saying about a common experience. **Underline** an adage. Use context to explain its meaning.

_____

_____

_____

_____

Paragraphs 2–7

Cause and Effect

Circle the text that tells the reason there are two guests instead of four.

Reread

Author's Craft

Who narrates the story? Explain why the author might have chosen this point of view.

FIND TEXT EVIDENCE 🔍

Read

Paragraphs 1–2

Make Predictions

Do you think a doctor will come? Explain your prediction.

_____

_____

Paragraphs 3–7

Cause and Effect

Underline text that shows Abby is anxious about finding the fever herbs to help Nellis.

Paragraphs 8–9

Dialect

Who does "the Missus" refer to? **Circle** clues. Write the answer here.

_____

Reread

Author's Craft

How does the author help you understand the risk Abby and Papa are taking?

Come morning, afore I entered the attic, I couldn't help **eavesdropping** on the sound of choked coughing. Once inside, I shuddered when I saw Nellis's gaunt face—so ill she looked. "I fear it's the fever," she gasped.

I summoned Papa, pleading, "She needs a doctor!"

"Think of the risk," he scolded. "The new law allows slave catchers to come all this way north, and if we're found harboring Nellis and Emma—well, **retaliation** could be grave. We must tend to this ourselves."

"But I lack Mother's know-how for curing," I whispered.

"Back in Virginia, Nellis told me 'bout some fever herbs," Emma spoke up.

"You daren't go out, Emma," Papa cautioned, "but Abby can procure what you need." I felt near fainting, but he was resolved. "Remember," he said to me, "the fields have eyes, and the woods have ears. Take care how you act and speak, so as not to arouse suspicion."

I left in haste with my basket, rehearsing Emma's words about the needed herb. "Grows on edges of clearings, by streams or marshes . . . has dull white flowers, wrinkled leaves, and stout stem." My search seemed endless, but finally I spied some flowers seeming to match Emma's description. I plucked the plant and some familiar mint that I knew for sure by its smell.

As I hurried home, I met our neighbor Mr. Carrington coming opposite. "Where to in such a hurry, Miss Abigail?"

Undaunted, I spun a tale about hunting up mint for Mother's special cake recipe, and my voice was wondrous calm as I presented a sprig ". . . for the Missus." Once he'd nodded thanks and continued on, I commenced to breathe again.

At home, Emma praised my harvest as she sorted through the leaves in the basket, handing me several and bidding me to mince them fine. Then she smiled. "Mint—that's good. We'll add some to mend the taste of the fever tea."

After Nellis drank the tea, she reclined in a comfortable doze. Emma and I watched over her, and before long we fell into voicing our worries. My own desperation from missing Mother was deeply felt and true, but I could barely fathom Emma's **fortitude** in facing the **rigors** of slavery as she tell'd them. I confessed my doubt of ever being able to bear such hardships as those.

"It's why folks come together. Problems shared be problems halved," said Emma smiling. "You'll soon enough have the strength of a grown lady like your mama."

Nellis's fever broke that night. As she and Emma prepared to continue their journey, they pledged **infinite** gratitude to Papa and me. Tho' sad to see them go, I wished them safe passage, and I thanked Emma for aiding me so in my own journey.

Summarize

Use your notes to orally summarize the story. In your summary, briefly describe the most important events and how the characters react to them.

FIND TEXT EVIDENCE 🔍

Read

Paragraph 1

Make Predictions

Will the tea help? Why or why not?

_____

_____

Paragraphs 2–4

Cause and Effect

How does her talk with Emma affect Abby? **Underline** evidence.

_____

_____

Reread

Author's Craft

What idea does the word *journey* in the last sentence represent?

Fluency

Read a paragraph to a partner. Adjust your rate to sound natural.

Vocabulary

Use the example sentences to talk with a partner about each word. Then answer the questions.

disposed

My brother is often **disposed** to eat pizza, since it is one of his favorite foods.

What is something you are disposed to do in your free time?

_____

_____

eavesdropping

Shayna learned about her surprise party by **eavesdropping** on her friends.

Why might someone be eavesdropping?

_____

_____

fortitude

It takes great **fortitude** to run a marathon.

What other tasks does it take fortitude to accomplish?

_____

_____

infinite

There seems to be an **infinite** number of stars in the night sky.

What is a synonym for _infinite_?

_____

_____

retaliation

Even though Ryan had poked me with his elbow, my teacher says it was not right to tap him with my pencil in **retaliation**.

What is another word for _retaliation_?

_____

_____

Build Your Word List Pick a word you found interesting in the selection you read. Look up synonyms and antonyms of the word in a print or digital thesaurus and write them in your writer's notebook.

rigors

The **rigors** of soccer practice left Peter exhausted.

What kind of rigors might an athlete face?

_____

_____

_____

stoop

On nice days, we like to sit on the front **stoop** of my house.

What is the purpose of a stoop?

_____

_____

_____

undaunted

Undaunted by the steep hill, the hikers continued along the trail.

When have you felt undaunted?

_____

_____

Adages and Proverbs

Adages and proverbs are traditional sayings that people use to express a widely accepted statement about life. They can contain colorful or figurative language.

🔍 FIND TEXT EVIDENCE

On page 36 of "Journey to Freedom," I'm not sure of the meaning of the fields have eyes, and the woods have ears. _But then Papa says that Abby must be careful "not to arouse suspicion," so I know he is warning her of danger. Personifying the fields and woods by giving them eyes and ears makes the warning easier to remember._

> "Remember," he said to me, "the fields have eyes, and the woods have ears. Take care how you act and speak, so as not to arouse suspicion."

Your Turn Use context clues to determine the meaning of the saying "Problems shared be problems halved" on page 37 of "Journey to Freedom."

_____

_____

_____

Make Predictions

When you read historical fiction, use clues in the text and knowledge you have gathered from other reading to make predictions, or logical guesses, about what a character from the past might do. As you read further, **confirm** or **revise** your predictions using evidence from the text.

🔍 **FIND TEXT EVIDENCE**

You may not have been sure how Abby would react when Papa asked her to find the herb. Reread paragraphs 6 and 7 on page 36 of "Journey to Freedom."

Page 36

> I left in haste with my basket, rehearsing Emma's words about the needed herb. "Grows on edges of clearings, by streams or marshes . . . has dull white flowers, wrinkled leaves, and stout stem." My search seemed endless, but finally I spied some flowers seeming to match Emma's description.

I predicted that Abby would do her best to find the herb, even though she felt unsure. I confirmed my prediction when I read that she rehearsed "Emma's words about the needed herb" and that she used them to select a plant "seeming to match Emma's description."

Your Turn What did you predict Abby would do when she met her neighbor on the way home? Explain how you then confirmed or revised your prediction. _____

_____

_____

Quick Tip

A good prediction is always supported by evidence, but the prediction can still be wrong. Stopping to think about why your prediction was incorrect is a great way to monitor your own understanding of a story's plot and characters. This will also help you make more accurate predictions as you continue to read.

Dialect

"Journey to Freedom" is historical fiction. Historical fiction is set in an actual place in the past. The characters face problems real people faced in the past. Historical fiction may include dialect, a way people speak in a certain time and place. It may also use characters' letters to develop the plot.

 FIND TEXT EVIDENCE

"Journey to Freedom" has a realistic setting from history. The dialect Abby uses in narrating the story and in her dialogue helps me to imagine a real Massachusetts girl in 1851. The letter that Abby reads provides information important to the plot.

Readers to Writers

While dialect makes your characters' words sound more authentic and true to a particular place and time, it can also be difficult for readers to interpret. Make sure to include context clues that help readers understand what the characters are saying.

Page 35

It is early summer 1851, and 12-year-old Abigail Parker is still finding her way after the death of her mother the previous winter. Her father has recently made their Massachusetts farm a station on the Underground Railroad, and the two nervously await their first "delivery" of people on their way to Canada to escape slavery.

I could not sit for being so fretful, so I paced and sometimes paused to peer out the window. Mother often said, "Patience is bitter, but its fruit is sweet." If only I were possessed of her calm.

"I see no sign of our four guests," Papa announced as he returned from checking outdoors, fueling my fears that they had met with misfortune. Just then, a sudden knock sounded, and my heart took to pounding as Papa opened the door to two weary women on the **stoop**. He assisted the older one, who appeared to be about 60, to a chair by the hearth. Her companion was maybe 14. Papa directed me to poke up the fire and fetch food and drink.

When the women got back their breath, Papa asked, "What of the others? Did they not accompany you?"

"Just Nellis and me," the girl declared, and the older woman presented a letter.

Papa handed the crumpled paper to me, saying, "If you would, Abby. My eyes fail me in dim light."

I brought the letter close by a candle and commenced reading:
"Dear Jonathan,

*I send you Nellis and Emma, separate from their two companions, who have fallen ill with fever, one seriously. We have insufficient room to hide four until they recover, so I hope you are **disposed** to shelter them until further transport can be arranged. Respectfully, Jacob."*

Papa nodded and said, "We must see to their safety and comfort." I guided them to the attic hiding place and wished them a peaceful night.

Dialect

A character's style of speech or narration reflects the way people spoke in the historical setting.

Letters

A letter from one character to another affects events in the plot.

Your Turn Find another example of dialect in "Journey to Freedom" and tell what it means. Then explain why an author might include dialect in historical fiction.

_____

_____

_____

Cause and Effect

When reading fiction, you learn about the **characters** from their responses to key events in the **plot**. As you read a story, pay attention to how each event causes one or more of the characters to react, as well as how each event and reaction develops the plot.

 FIND TEXT EVIDENCE

As I reread the beginning of "Journey to Freedom," I note that the knock at the door causes Abby's heart to start pounding. I can infer from this reaction that she is nervous.

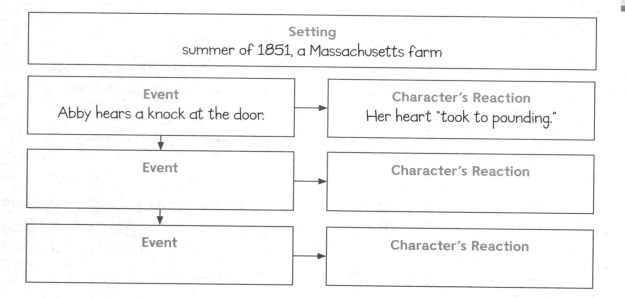

Setting
summer of 1851, a Massachusetts farm

Event	Character's Reaction
Abby hears a knock at the door.	Her heart "took to pounding."
Event	Character's Reaction
Event	Character's Reaction

 Your Turn Show how the story's plot develops by using the graphic organizer on page 43 to record additional events and the reactions they cause in one or more of the characters.

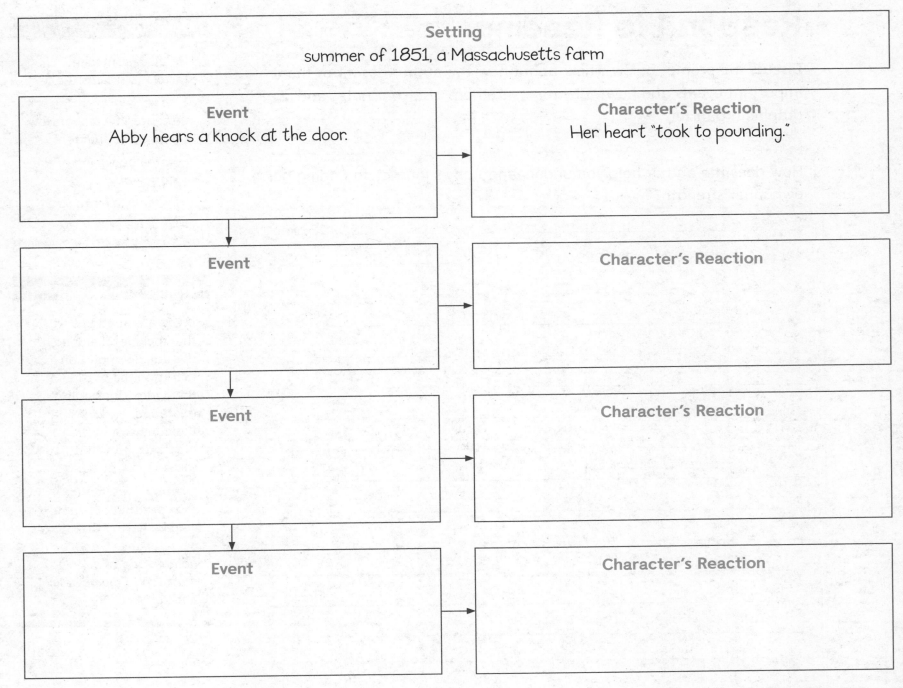

Setting
summer of 1851, a Massachusetts farm

Event
Abby hears a knock at the door.

Character's Reaction
Her heart "took to pounding."

Event

Character's Reaction

Event

Character's Reaction

Event

Character's Reaction

Respond to Reading

Discuss the prompt below. Think about how the author describes the important events and how Abby reacts to them. Use your notes and graphic organizer.

How does the author help you understand Abby's journey to finding her own inner strength?

_____
_____
_____
_____
_____
_____
_____
_____
_____
_____
_____
_____
_____

Quick Tip

Use these sentence starters to discuss the text and to organize ideas.

- *The story's point of view allows the author to . . .*
- *At the beginning of the story, Abby . . .*
- *By the end, readers learn . . .*

Grammar Connections

If you are quoting text that includes dialogue, use double quotation marks on the outside of the quote. Use single quotation marks inside the double quotation marks to show that someone is speaking.

Example: The author shows that Papa wants to help by having the narrator say, *"Papa nodded and said, 'We must see to their safety and comfort.'"*

Paraphrasing Sources

When you paraphrase, you restate information in your own words. **Paraphrasing source information** is not the same as summarizing, or stating only the most important ideas. When you paraphrase, you include more details than when you summarize, and you let your own voice come through. To paraphrase a source

- make sure you understand the information before you begin;
- restate ideas using synonyms and familiar language;
- use easier sentence structures to clarify ideas.

Why would you choose to paraphrase rather than summarize a source?

_____

_____

Create a Pamphlet With a group, research the exhibits in the Smithsonian National Museum of African American History and Culture. Take notes by paraphrasing the information you find in your sources, as well as using direct quotes when appropriate. Remember to credit your sources. Then create a pamphlet with information about one of the exhibits. Consider these questions as you plan your pamphlet:

- What does this exhibit help me understand about life in America?
- Why is this exhibit important for people to see?
- What is the most interesting way to present the information?

Also discuss the photographs, captions, and other visual elements you will include. You will be sharing your pamphlet with your classmates.

First opened to the public in 2016, the National Museum of African American History and Culture contains more than 36,000 artifacts that help tell the story of African American life and history.

Michael Ventura/Alamy Stock Photo

Elijah of Buxton

 How does the author help you visualize how Elijah feels?

 Talk About It Reread **Literature Anthology** page 353. Talk with a partner about what is happening to Elijah and how he feels.

Cite Text Evidence How does the author help you visualize how Elijah feels? Write text evidence in the chart and tell what you visualize.

Text Evidence	What I Visualize

Write The author helps me visualize how Elijah feels by _____

_____

_____

Literature Anthology: pages 350–365

Quick Tip

When you visualize, you use descriptive words and phrases to picture what something is like. As you reread, think about what words and phrases help you imagine how someone is feeling.

How does the author use dialogue to help you understand the relationship between Ma and Elijah?

Talk About It Reread the first five paragraphs on **Literature Anthology** page 358. Talk about how Elijah feels about what Ma says.

Cite Text Evidence How does the dialogue and Elijah's narration help you understand what Ma and Elijah are thinking? Write text evidence in the chart.

Reread the first five paragraphs on **Literature Anthology** page 358.

Ma Says	Elijah Says	What I Understand

Write The author helps me see the relationship between Ma and Elijah by

_____

_____

_____

Quick Tip

Dialect is how certain people of a time and place spoke. If you find it difficult to understand the dialect, try reading the text aloud. Hearing dialect pronounced aloud often makes it easier to comprehend.

How does the author show that Elijah's character is growing?

Talk About It Reread the last six paragraphs of the story on **Literature Anthology** page 364. Talk with a partner about Elijah's experience with the women.

Cite Text Evidence What descriptive language does the author use to show how Elijah sees and experiences the women's support? Write text evidence in the chart.

Evaluate Information

Elijah compares the women bunching up around Mrs. Holton to a ring of soldiers that no sorrow could "bust through." What can you infer about the women and how they make Elijah feel?

Text Evidence

↓

What This Shows

Write I know Elijah is growing because the author _____

_____

_____

Respond to Reading

COLLABORATE

Discuss the prompt below. Think about how Elijah responds to what happens around him and to what people in the story say. Use your notes and graphic organizer.

Think about Elijah's transformation from boyhood to adolescence. How does the author show Elijah's inner strength on his journey to adulthood?

_____
_____
_____
_____
_____
_____
_____
_____
_____
_____
_____
_____

Self-Selected Reading

Choose a text and fill in your writer's notebook with the title, author, and genre. Include a personal response to the text in your writer's notebook. If you choose historical fiction, jot down your thoughts on the time period and place in which the story is set, along with what the story helped you understand about what it might have been like to live in that time and place.

The People Could Fly

*Literature Anthology:
pages 368–371*

? How does the illustration help you understand how the people in the folktale felt?

Talk About It Look at the illustration on **Literature Anthology** page 368. Talk with a partner about how the people look and what they are doing.

Cite Text Evidence What details in the illustration help you understand how flying made the people feel? Write them in the chart.

Illustration	What It Means

Quick Tip

Details in an illustration can help set a story's mood, or the feeling the story creates in a reader. As you analyze the illustration, think about how the details make you feel. Then connect that mood to the feelings of the characters in the story.

Write The illustration helps me understand that the people in the folktale

_____

_____

_____

? **How does the author help you understand what working was like for the enslaved people?**

COLLABORATE

Talk About It Reread the sixth paragraph on **Literature Anthology** page 369. Talk with a partner about what kind of person the Master is.

Cite Text Evidence How does the author help you understand how the enslaved people are treated? Write text evidence.

Evaluate Information

Notice that Virginia Hamilton describes the Master using short, choppy sentence fragments. Why do you think she does this? What is the effect of these short descriptions?

Text Evidence

↓

What I Understand

Write The author helps readers understand the terrible oppression and treatment of enslaved people by _____

_____

_____

How does the author help you visualize Sarah's flight?

Talk About It Reread the third and fourth paragraphs on **Literature Anthology** page 370. Talk with a partner about how Sarah flies.

Cite Text Evidence How does the author describe how Sarah takes flight? Write text evidence in the chart.

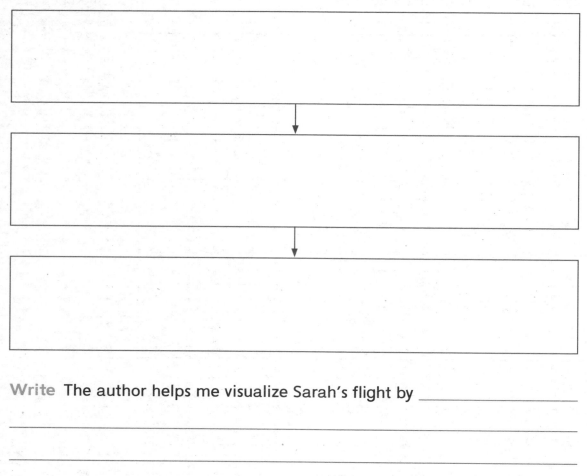

Write The author helps me visualize Sarah's flight by _____

_____

_____

_____

Author's Purpose

Everything in a well-written story is there for a purpose, or reason. This includes not only information, but also the exact language the author uses and how he or she uses it. Authors think about the effects of their chosen words and make sure the words help tell the story the author wants to tell.

FIND TEXT EVIDENCE

In paragraph 3 on page 370 of "The People Could Fly," the author uses the sentence fragment "As light as a feather" to describe Sarah rising and escaping. Authors sometimes use sentence fragments to emphasize a point or to focus on an image.

Your Turn Reread paragraph 3 on page 370.

- What is the effect of the fragment "As light as a feather"?

  _____

  _____

  _____

  _____

- Now reread the rest of page 370 and find another fragment. What is

  its effect? _____

  _____

  _____

  _____

If you are unsure why an author uses certain words or sentence structures, think about their effect. Ask:

- What do they tell you about the characters, plot, or setting?
- What kind of mood or tone do they create?

The answers to these questions will tell you what the author's purpose is. When you write, make sure you have a reason for the language you choose.

MAKE CONNECTIONS

Text Connections

? **How do the lyrics of "Lift Every Voice and Sing" and the descriptions in *Elijah of Buxton* and "The People Could Fly" help you understand the characters' inner strength?**

COLLABORATE

Talk About It Read the lyrics. Talk with a partner about how James Weldon Johnson shares how he feels.

Cite Text Evidence **Underline** words and phrases that work together to convey the theme of inner strength.

Write The song lyrics and stories I read help me understand _____

_____

_____

_____

_____

_____

Quick Tip

Take turns reading the song aloud with your partner. After each verse, stop and tell what you visualize happening. What actions show inner strength?

Lift Every Voice and Sing

Lift ev'ry voice and sing, till earth and heaven ring,
Ring with the harmonies of liberty.
Let our rejoicing rise high as the list'ning skies,
Let it resound loud as the rolling sea.

Sing a song full of the faith that the dark past has taught us;
Sing a song full of the hope that the present has brought us;
Facing the rising sun of our new day begun,
Let us march on till victory is won.

— **James Weldon Johnson**

Published just thirty-five years after the official end of slavery, this African American song celebrates freedom.

Present Your Work

COLLABORATE

Discuss how you will present your pamphlet about an exhibit at the National Museum of African American History and Culture. Use the Listening Checklist as your classmates give their presentations. Then discuss the sentence starters below and write your answers.

Tech Tip

Once you've collected images for your pamphlet, consider using photo editing software to enhance the images by adding effects or resizing to fit a specific area on your pamphlet.

The Smithsonian National Museum of African American History and Culture

✓ Listening Checklist

☐ Listen actively by taking notes on the ideas presented.

☐ Pay attention to nonverbal cues, such as pointing and other gestures, given by the presenter.

☐ Politely alert the presenter if you are having trouble hearing him or her or viewing materials.

☐ Ask relevant questions and make pertinent comments about the presentation.

An interesting fact I learned about an exhibit at the National Museum of African American History and Culture is _____

_____

I would like to know more about _____

_____

_____

Talk About It

Essential Question

How have tools used for exploration evolved over time?

You may be familiar with snorkeling or scuba diving. But have you ever seen anyone explore the ocean like this? The person in this photo is using a sub-scooter to get close to sea creatures in their natural habitats in the Indian Ocean. The application of submarine technology to the familiar design of a scooter allows the person using the sub-scooter to move and discover at his or her own pace.

Look at the photograph. Talk to a partner about what you see. Discuss what you know about the improvement of tools used for exploration. Write your ideas in the web.

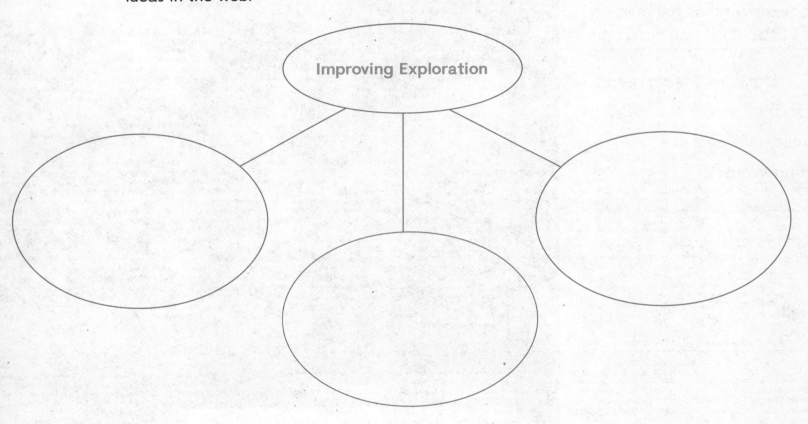

Improving Exploration

Go online to **my.mheducation.com** and read the "Radio's Scariest Hour" Blast. Think about popular science-fiction movies or stories you've seen or are familiar with. What might scientists be able to find in real life through space exploration? Then blast back your response.

Holger Leue/Lonely Planet Images/Getty Images

TIME FOR KIDS.

TAKE NOTES

Before you begin reading, preview the title, headings, and images. Make a prediction about what you think you will learn. Write your prediction here, and remember to confirm or correct it as you read.

_____

_____

_____

As you read, take note of

Interesting Words _____

_____

_____

Key Details _____

_____

_____

_____

_____

Essential Question

?

How have tools used for exploration evolved over time?

Read how advances in technology have aided exploration.

A sextant can still be used today to navigate at sea.

(l)Thomas J. Abercrombie/National Geographic/Getty Images, (r)A. Gomez/Flickr/Getty Images; (bkgrd)Jeff Spielman/Photodisc/Getty Images

Tools of the
Explorer's Trade

The word *technology* sounds modern, but people have been using it for at least 300 years! Considering that one definition of *technology* is "the use of knowledge for practical purposes," we can say people have been developing new technologies since the dawn of human history. Some of them are antiquated. Others are continually improved. Stone Age axes qualify as technology, as do the wheel and the telephone. The following survey of historical navigation techniques is one example of how innovative technologies evolve over time.

The North Star

Sailors of early civilizations were creative thinkers. They used the star Polaris, also called the North Star, to get their bearings at sea. But using the North Star had some serious drawbacks. First, it can only be seen on clear nights, so attempting to navigate through unknown waters on a cloudy night could be **catastrophic.** Second, Polaris can be seen only from the Northern Hemisphere. While navigating with the North Star was useful under certain circumstances, something better was needed.

The Astrolabe

The astrolabe was an advanced measuring tool invented in the Middle East. Though its primary **application** was to make **computations** about time and the positions of the Sun, Moon, planets, and stars, it was also employed as a technological aid to navigation. The thoughtfully designed astrolabe gave mariners a way to determine the latitude of their ships while at sea.

A Moorish astrolabe made in Andalusia, Spain

ARGUMENTATIVE TEXT

FIND TEXT EVIDENCE

Read

Paragraph 1

Summarize

Summarize the information in this paragraph.

_____

_____

_____

_____

Paragraphs 2–3

Author's Point of View

Draw a box around the sentence that best expresses how the author feels about the use of the North Star as a navigational tool.
Underline clues that tell how the author feels about the astrolabe.

Reread

Author's Craft

Why are the headings an important part of the text's organization?

SHARED READ

FIND TEXT EVIDENCE

Read

Paragraph 1 and Sextant Diagram
Evaluate Information

Underline the information in the paragraph that the diagram best helps explain.

Paragraph 2, Photograph, and Caption
Summarize

Summarize what made the invention of the compass important.

_____

_____

_____

_____

_____

_____

_____

Reread

Author's Craft

Why do you think the author includes a diagram and photographs?

The Sextant

The sextant is another fantastic tool that used the positions of the Sun and stars to find a location on Earth. First developed in Asia Minor in the late tenth century, it was used to measure the angle between a celestial object and the horizon. When navigators considered the measurement in relation to the time of day or night it was taken, they could find their ship's location on a nautical chart. Far from **obsolete,** this technology is still used today as a backup to modern navigation technologies!

The Compass

A compass is made by balancing a **magnetic** needle above a circular dial. Earth's own strong magnetic field causes the needle to swing into a north-south position. Because a compass indicates direction in all weather and at all times of the day or night, its importance as a navigational technology was quickly recognized. Historians are unsure who invented the compass, but we do know it was in use in China as early as the eleventh century.

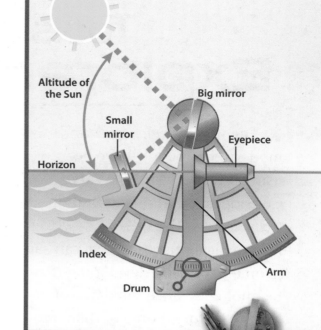

Altitude of the Sun

Big mirror

Small mirror

Eyepiece

Horizon

Index

Arm

Drum

A sextant (right) and how it measures angles (above)

(c) Burke/Triolo/Brand X Pictures/Jupiterimages; (b) William Whitehurst/Corbis; (bkgd) Jeff Spielman/Photodisc/Getty Images

A compass uses Earth's magnetic field to show direction.

An Opinion: Let's Keep Looking

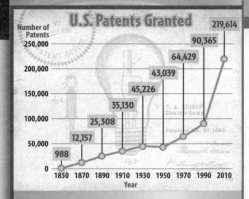

Many characterize the ongoing story of human exploration as one of courage and creative resourcefulness. For most of history, exploration was confined to Earth's surface. But in 1930, we began diving into the ocean's depths. By 1969, we had landed on the moon. The probes that we **deployed** into deep space in 1977 are still transmitting valuable data back to us across billions of miles. **Subsequently,** we have sent robotic vehicles to survey the surface of Mars. And we have a powerful telescope in orbit that is sending us spectacular photographs of the formation of distant stars.

Exploring the unknown has clearly fueled our inventiveness, but it also inspires our imaginations. Because we are constantly **elevating** our aspirations, we have been able to increase our knowledge even when expectations have been the worst. Modern technologies are providing more and better tools to explore increasingly remote places. In fact, when it comes to exploration, the best is certainly yet to come. We should always resist the idea that an adventurous instinct might be foolhardy, and we should continue to value and encourage curiosity.

U.S. Patents Granted

Year	Number of Patents
1850	988
1870	12,157
1890	25,308
1910	35,130
1930	45,226
1950	43,039
1970	64,429
1990	90,365
2010	219,614

Inventing as Fast as We Can

When the U.S. government grants patents to "promote the Progress of Science and useful Arts," it gives exclusive rights to inventors for a set period of time. The number of patents issued in the years from 1850 to 2010 reveals a stunning increase in the rate of technological innovations.

Summarize

Use your notes to summarize aloud the important information in "Tools of the Explorer's Trade." Then discuss the prediction you made on page 58. Determine whether or not your prediction was correct and why.

ARGUMENTATIVE TEXT

FIND TEXT EVIDENCE 🔍

Read

Sidebar (Paragraphs 1-2)
Author's Point of View

Underline text that shows a point of view. What is that point of view?

_____

_____

Graphs

What do you learn from the graph?

_____

_____

Connotations and Denotations

Does *stunning* give a positive or negative feeling? **Circle** clues that help you decide.

_____

Reread

Author's Craft

How does the author use facts about the past and present to support an argument about the future?

Vocabulary

Use the example sentences to talk with a partner about each word. Then answer the questions.

application

The instructions for putting up a tent seemed easy, but their **application** was difficult.

What activities would likely require the application of instructions?

_____

_____

catastrophic

Our class raised money to help rebuild homes destroyed by the **catastrophic** tornado.

What is a synonym of *catastrophic?*

_____

_____

computations

We performed **computations** to figure out how much our budget should be for the school play.

What is a tool commonly used to perform computations?

_____

_____

deployed

Firefighters were **deployed** to look for the cause of the fire.

Why might extra police officers be deployed during a parade?

_____

_____

elevating

One of the doctor's recommendations was **elevating** the patient's leg while it healed.

When might a doctor recommend elevating your leg?

_____

_____

Build Your Word List Pick a word you found interesting in the selection you read. Look up the word, its pronunciation and origin, and its definition in a print or digital dictionary. Write the information in your writer's notebook.

magnetic

Things with **magnetic** properties attract objects containing iron.

What items that you use have magnetic features?

_____

_____

_____

obsolete

Modern digital functions have replaced all kinds of older, **obsolete** technology.

What is an antonym of *obsolete?*

_____

_____

_____

subsequently

The team played well all season and **subsequently** reached the playoffs.

If athletes had practiced all morning, what might they subsequently do?

_____

_____

_____

Connotations and Denotations

The **denotation** of a word is its dictionary definition. The **connotations** of a word are associations it has that are beyond its basic meaning. Context can help you identify a word's connotation.

 FIND TEXT EVIDENCE

I see the word antiquated *on page 59 of "Tools of the Explorer's Trade." Its definition, or denotation, is "out of date." Here* antiquated *has a negative connotation because the author contrasts antiquated technologies with other "continually improved" technologies.*

Some of them are antiquated. Others are continually improved.

Your Turn Decide if the following words from "Tools of the Explorer's Trade" have a negative or positive connotation. What context clues help you know this?

evolve, *page 59* _____

_____

spectacular, *page 61* _____

_____

Summarize

Summarizing a text can help you understand the information in it. As you read "Tools of the Explorer's Trade," identify the key ideas about technologies used for exploration. Use the ideas to summarize the text in your own words.

🔍 FIND TEXT EVIDENCE

You may not be sure how to summarize the significance of the sextant as a tool for exploration. Reread the section "The Sextant" on page 60 of "Tools of the Explorer's Trade."

Page 60

> The sextant is another fantastic tool that used the positions of the Sun and stars to find a location on Earth. First developed in Asia Minor in the late tenth century, it was used to measure the angle between a celestial object and the horizon. When navigators considered the measurement in relation to the time of day or night it was taken, they could find their ship's location on a nautical chart. Far from **obsolete**, this technology is still used today as a backup to modern navigation technologies!

I read details about taking angle measurements and using them to find a "ship's location," both in the past and as a "backup" today. To summarize this section, I can say that an old tool, the sextant, still has value as a navigational technology.

Your Turn Reread the section "The Astrolabe" on page 59 to identify the key ideas. Then use them to summarize how the astrolabe helped mariners.

_____

_____

_____

To keep your summary short, make sure that you include only the most important main ideas and supporting details from the text. As you take notes for your summary, check for extra details, and cross them out if they are not needed.

Sidebars and Graphs

"Tools of the Explorer's Trade" is an argumentative text that supports the author's claims about a topic with valid reasons and evidence. Argumentative texts may include graphs to represent concepts visually and sidebars to present more opinions related to the topic.

 FIND TEXT EVIDENCE

"Tools of the Explorer's Trade" includes a sidebar about the benefits of exploration and a graph that makes an additional point related to the topic.

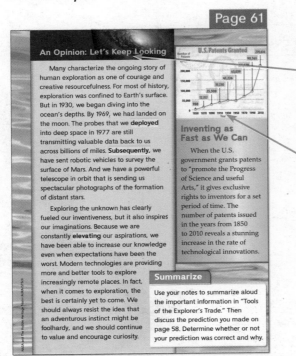

Page 61

An Opinion: Let's Keep Looking

Many characterize the ongoing story of human exploration as one of courage and creative resourcefulness. For most of history, exploration was confined to Earth's surface. But in 1930, we began diving into the ocean's depths. By 1969, we had landed on the moon. The probes that we **deployed** into deep space in 1977 are still transmitting valuable data back to us across billions of miles. **Subsequently,** we have sent robotic vehicles to survey the surface of Mars. And we have a powerful telescope in orbit that is sending us spectacular photographs of the formation of distant stars.

Exploring the unknown has clearly fueled our inventiveness, but it also inspires our imaginations. Because we are constantly **elevating** our aspirations, we have been able to increase our knowledge even when expectations have been the worst. Modern technologies are providing more and better tools to explore increasingly remote places. In fact, when it comes to exploration, the best is certainly yet to come. We should always resist the idea that an adventurous instinct might be foolhardy, and we should continue to value and encourage curiosity.

U.S. Patents Granted

Inventing as Fast as We Can

When the U.S. government grants patents to "promote the Progress of Science and useful Arts," it gives exclusive rights to inventors for a set period of time. The number of patents issued in the years from 1850 to 2010 reveals a stunning increase in the rate of technological innovations.

Summarize

Use your notes to summarize aloud the important information in "Tools of the Explorer's Trade." Then discuss the prediction you made on page 58. Determine whether or not your prediction was correct and why.

Sidebars

Sidebars add relevant information, such as an opinion related to the topic.

Graphs

Graphs of numerical data often show how something has changed over time.

Your Turn Explain how the sidebar and graph on page 61 add to your understanding of the topic of "Tools of the Explorer's Trade."

_____

_____

_____

_____

Readers to Writers

When including graphs in your writing, make sure you use one that suits your purpose.

- A bar graph makes it easy to compare numerical values.
- A line graph shows how numerical values change over time.
- A circle graph, or pie chart, shows how smaller amounts or percentages of something compare to the total.

Author's Point of View

In an argumentative text, an **author's point of view** is the claim, or position, an author presents about a topic. Strong claims are supported with credible reasons and valid text evidence. To identify the author's point of view, analyze his or her choice of words as well as the reasons and evidence the author provides.

🔍 FIND TEXT EVIDENCE

When I reread "Tools of the Explorer's Trade," I can look for details that suggest a particular perspective on tools used for exploration.

Details	Author's Point of View
People have always sought and created new technologies.	
Using the North Star to navigate was not best.	

Burke/Triolo/Brand X Pictures/Jupiterimages

Quick Tip

Pay attention to the author's word choice in an argumentative text. Is he or she describing something in a negative or a positive way? Words such as *fantastic* and *better* are positive. Words such as *drawbacks* and *worst* are negative.

Your Turn Reread "Tools of the Explorer's Trade." List additional key details in the graphic organizer on page 67 that support the author's point of view. Then state the point of view in the right hand column.

Details	Author's Point of View
People have always sought and created new technologies.	
Using the North Star to navigate was not best.	

Respond to Reading

COLLABORATE

Discuss the prompt below. Think about how the author presents the information. Use your notes and graphic organizer.

How does the author use text organization and text features to convey how navigational technology has evolved over time?

_____

_____

_____

_____

_____

_____

_____

_____

_____

_____

_____

_____

_____

Quick Tip

Use these sentence starters to discuss the text and organize your ideas:

- *The author uses . . . to organize the text. This helps readers because . . .*

- *Text features help readers understand . . .*

- *The author shares an opinion about evolving technology by . . .*

Grammar Connections

Names of specific places on Earth or in space, such as the North Star, are capitalized. As you write your response, make sure to capitalize place names correctly. For instance:

It could be seen from the Northern Hemisphere.

The compass was used in China.

Evaluate Sources

As part of any research project, you must **evaluate your sources** to make sure they are reliable and can be trusted. To evaluate a particular print or digital source, ask yourself these questions:

- Does the source come from a reputable authority, such as a museum, government, or educational institution?
- Is the information the source provides up-to-date?
- Does the source contain bias? Does it seem to favor a specific approach or opinion?

How might you answer one of the questions above?

_____

_____

Make a Timeline With a group, create a timeline tracking the development of tools used for space exploration, such as spacesuits, space food, and safety tethers. Consider the following:

- What tools have advanced space exploration, and when was each invented?
- At what date should your timeline begin? When should it end?
- What intervals, or spaces between dates, will you mark on your timeline?

As part of your timeline, create a works cited page listing the sources you used in your research. Also discuss what visuals you might add to your timeline. You will be sharing your timeline with your classmates.

Quick Tip

Your works cited page should include a citation for each source that has contributed to your final work. Include the following information in each entry:

- title of source
- author's name
- publisher or website URL
- publication or copyright date

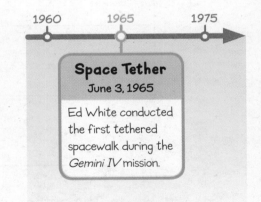

1960   1965   1975

Space Tether
June 3, 1965

Ed White conducted the first tethered spacewalk during the *Gemini IV* mission.

The image above shows a part of a timeline about tools used in space exploration.

Out of This World

? How does the graph help you understand the importance of the space shuttle program?

Literature Anthology: pages 372–375

Talk About It Reread **Literature Anthology** page 373 and analyze the graph. Talk with a partner about technology and the space program.

Cite Text Evidence What evidence from the graph shows the frequency of missions flown by the space shuttle fleet? Write evidence in the chart. What does this help you understand?

 Make Inferences

The text says that one of the six shuttles, *Enterprise,* was used for training and never actually flew a mission. Think of the costs associated with developing and maintaining a space shuttle that would never be deployed. What does the fact that there was a shuttle only used for training help you understand?

Evidence	What I Understand

Write The author uses a graph to help me see the importance of the space shuttle program by _____

_____

? **How does the timeline support the author's message about evolving technology?**

Talk About It Analyze the timeline on **Literature Anthology** page 374. Talk with a partner about how the timeline helps you understand the events of space exploration.

Cite Text Evidence What clues in the timeline tell about how technology has evolved? Use the timeline to add additional information about the events named in the chart.

1957 for first satellite launch

↓

1961 for first person into space

↓

1962 for John Glenn

↓

2003 for Mars Rovers

Write I understand the author's message about evolving technology

because the timeline _____

_____

_____

Respond to Reading

COLLABORATE

Discuss the prompt below. Think about how the author presents information about the evolution of space exploration. Use your notes and graphic organizer.

How does the author use text features to help you understand the evolving technology used in the space program?

_____

_____

_____

_____

_____

_____

_____

_____

_____

_____

_____

_____

Self-Selected Reading

Choose a text to read independently. Reading for a longer length of time without interruption will help you develop a stronger connection to a topic. Read the first two pages. If five or more words are unfamiliar, you may decide to choose another text. Fill in your writer's notebook with the title, author, and genre. Include a personal response to the text.

Space Shuttles on the Move

Literature Anthology: pages 376–377

1   When NASA's space shuttle program ended in 2011, a decision had to be made. What should be done with some of the spaceships that had been taking off from Cape Canaveral in Florida since 1981? One newspaper made a few computations about the space shuttle *Discovery*, and made it sound as if NASA were selling a used car: "27 years old, 150 million miles traveled, somewhat damaged but well maintained. Price: $0. Dealer preparation and destination charges: $28.8 million."

Circle the sentence in the first paragraph that helps you know what NASA officials needed to decide. Paraphrase it here:

_____

_____

_____

2   Damaged or not, civic leaders, museum workers, and space buffs in 29 cities around the country eagerly awaited NASA's decision about where *Discovery* would end up. The space shuttles *Endeavor, Atlantis,* and *Enterprise* were also ending their careers in space, and their final destinations also had to be decided.

Reread paragraph 2. Talk with a partner about who wanted to know where the retired space shuttles would end up. **Underline** text evidence.

The retired space shuttles are on display at various locations around the United States.

Intrepid Sea, Air & Space Museum/AP Images

How do the illustrations and captions help you better understand what happens to retired space shuttles?

Talk About It Look at the illustration on page 73. Talk with a partner about what communities might do with a space shuttle.

Cite Text Evidence What clues in the illustration and caption help show what happens when space shuttles are retired? Write evidence in the chart. Then write the author's purpose for including this information.

Clues	Author's Purpose

Write The author uses illustrations and captions to help me _____

_____

_____

_____

Problem and Solution

Text structure refers to how an author organizes ideas or information. Authors can use a **problem and solution** text structure to help readers understand why something is a problem and how the problem was solved or could be solved. The information about the problem and its solution helps the author support a main idea.

A problem and solution structure can keep readers interested in the topic. Once the problem is presented, readers will be curious to read on to learn how it was or could be solved.

Readers to Writers

FIND TEXT EVIDENCE

In paragraph 1 of "Space Shuttles on the Move" on page 73, the author says "a decision had to be made," and then asks a question. These clues, along with the phrase *what should be done with,* signal that the author is presenting a problem that must be solved.

> When NASA's space shuttle program ended in 2011, a decision had to be made. What should be done with some of the spaceships that had been taking off from Cape Canaveral in Florida since 1981?

Your Turn Reread paragraphs 1 and 2 and the caption on page 73.

- Explain how the author presents a solution to the problem set up in paragraph 1. _____

  _____

  _____

- What is the main idea of the text? _____

  _____

Text Connections

How does the tone of Emily Dickinson's poem "The Railway Train" compare to the tone presented in *Out of This World* **and "Space Shuttles on the Move"?**

Talk About It Read the poem "The Railway Train." Talk about the speaker's tone, or attitude toward the train. Keep in mind that when the poem was written, trains were a relatively new form of technology.

Cite Text Evidence **Circle** five examples where the train is compared to a living creature.

Write The tone of the poem is similar to the tone of the selections I read this week because like the selections _____

_____

_____

_____

_____

_____

_____

_____

The Railway Train

I like to see it lap the miles,
And lick the valleys up,
And stop to feed itself at tanks;
And then, prodigious, step

Around a pile of mountains,
And, supercilious, peer
In shanties by the sides of roads;
And then a quarry pare

To fit its sides, and crawl between,
Complaining all the while
In horrid, hooting stanza;
Then chase itself down hill

And neigh like Boanerges;
Then, punctual as a star,
Stop—docile and omnipotent—
At its own stable door.

— **Emily Dickinson**

Accuracy and Rate

To read argumentative texts with **accuracy**, make sure that you pronounce each word and number correctly. You may need to adjust your **rate**, or speed, to read more slowly so that you can pronounce all the words clearly and correctly.

Page 61

> But in 1930, we began diving into the ocean's depths.

Think about how you would read years in contrast to how you would read other numbers.

Think about how punctuation, such as commas, can help you adjust your rate.

Quick Tip

Before you begin reading, preview the text. If the text focuses on a science topic, look for specialized content words and words containing multiple syllables. Think of the correct pronunciation of each syllable of a multisyllabic word.

Your Turn Turn to page 61. Take turns reading aloud the first paragraph of the sidebar with a partner. Think about how to read the years as well as multisyllabic words such as *characterize* and *resourcefulness*. Plan your rate of reading so that you can read with accuracy.

Afterward, think about how you did. Complete these sentences.

I remembered to _____

_____

Next time, I will _____

_____

Expert Model

*Literature Anthology:
pages 372–375*

Features of an Opinion Essay

An opinion essay is a form of argumentative text. It states and supports the author's opinion, or point of view, on a topic. An opinion essay

- has a clearly communicated opinion, or claim, about a topic;

- includes valid reasons and relevant evidence that support the author's opinion;

- uses a variety of sentence structures to communicate ideas clearly and engage the reader.

Analyze an Expert Model Studying argumentative texts will help you plan and write an opinion essay. **Reread** the sidebar "Save Our Planet" on **Literature Anthology** page 375. Write your answers to the questions below.

What is the author's opinion about public funding for space research?

_____

_____

_____

Why does the author include the budgets for NASA, the Environmental Protection Agency, and the National Park Service? _____

_____

_____

Plan: Choose Your Topic

COLLABORATE

Freewrite Who should be in charge of space exploration—the government, private businesses, or a joint partnership? With a partner, discuss the benefits and disadvantages of each option. Then freewrite a paragraph summarizing your ideas on a separate sheet of paper.

Writing Prompt Write an opinion essay that states your point of view about whether space exploration should be led by the government, private businesses, or a joint partnership. Support your opinion with clear reasons and relevant evidence.

The point of view I will present in my opinion essay is _____

_____

_____

Purpose and Audience Think about your audience and purpose for writing. Then consider the language you will use in your essay.

My purpose for writing is to _____

My audience will be _____

I will use _____ language to write my essay.

Plan In your writer's notebook, make a Topic and Details web to plan your opinion essay. Write your topic in the Topic circle.

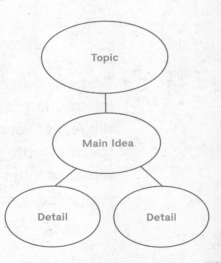

Topic

Main Idea

Detail   Detail

Plan: Strong Introduction

Write an Effective Introduction You will need to gather your information before you begin to write. The introduction is your chance to grab readers' attention with a surprising fact, statistic, quotation, or anecdote. Your introduction should identify your topic and state your position on an issue. As you plan and write your introduction, ask

• Is the topic clear to readers?

• Do I clearly state my claim and list reasons for my opinion?

• What interesting and relevant fact, quotation, anecdote, or statistic will grabs readers' attention?

Write an interesting fact, anecdote, quotation, or statistic that will get your reader's attention.

_____

_____

_____

_____

 Graphic Organizer Once you have decided what information to use to support your claim, fill in the rest of your web. If you need more space to write your details, use a separate sheet of paper in your writer's notebook.

FatCamera/Getty Images

Draft

Develop Support Authors of opinion essays support their claims and reasons with relevant evidence, such as facts, details, examples, and definitions. In the example below from a paragraph in "Hurtling Through Space from Home," the author offers examples to support the claim that "new and exciting discoveries are made" in astronomy.

> Every year, new and exciting discoveries are made. In six years, the Curiosity Rover has learned that water—and maybe life—once existed on Mars. NASA's Kepler mission has found 2,327 exoplanets, or planets outside our solar system, since it started in 2009.

Now use the example as a model for how to include supporting evidence in a paragraph for your own opinion essay. Draft your paragraph below.

_____

_____

_____

_____

_____

Write a Draft Use your Topic and Details web to help you write your draft in your writer's notebook. Remember to introduce your topic and claim in an engaging way.

Quick Tip

Keep in mind that a draft is only a first pass at your writing. You don't have to worry about making grammar, spelling, or organizational mistakes. There will be time to fix those later. The important thing is to get your ideas down on paper.

Revise

Sentence Structure Writing that contains only simple sentences can be repetitious and dull. Vary your sentence structure by combining simple sentences into compound sentences, or by adding a dependent clause to a simple sentence to create a complex sentence. Transition words can help connect ideas. Revise the paragraph below by varying the sentence structures to make the writing clearer and more interesting.

> The National Aeronautics and Space Administration (NASA) has existed since the 1960s. It has met seemingly impossible goals of getting people into space and back safely. Some people think NASA is obsolete. NASA has been involved in the International Space Station since 2000. It has been helping scientists learn about our universe.

Grammar Connections

Here are some examples of sentence types and transition words.

Simple sentences: *We climbed higher. The temperature dropped.*

A complex sentence with a dependent clause: *As we climbed higher, the temperature dropped.*

Transition words and phrases include *however, furthermore, similarly,* and *on the contrary.*

_____

_____

_____

_____

_____

Revise Revise your draft. Evaluate sentence structure to make sure your ideas are clear and your writing is interesting.

Peer Conferences

Review a Draft Listen carefully as a partner reads his or her work aloud. Take notes about what you liked and what was difficult to follow. Begin by telling what you liked about the draft. Ask questions that will help the writer think more about the writing. Make suggestions that you think will make the writing stronger. Use these sentence starters.

You did a good job of explaining why . . .

To make your introduction more engaging, you might . . .

Stronger evidence would better support the idea that . . .

Combining sentences would help readers understand . . .

Partner Feedback After your partner gives you feedback on your draft, write one of the suggestions that you will use in your revision. Refer to the rubric on page 85 as you give feedback.

Based on my partner's feedback, I will _____

_____

_____

After you finish giving each other feedback, reflect on the peer conference. What was helpful? What might you do differently next time?

Revision As you revise your draft, use the Revising Checklist to help you figure out what text you may need to move, elaborate on, or delete. Remember to use the rubric on page 85 to help you with your revision.

✓ Revising Checklist

☐ Does my writing fit my purpose and audience?

☐ Have I written a strong introduction that identifies my topic and states my claim clearly and in an engaging way?

☐ Do I need to add more reasons and evidence to support my claim?

☐ Does my writing contain a variety of sentence structures?

Edit and Proofread

When you **edit** and **proofread** your writing, you look for and correct mistakes in spelling, punctuation, capitalization, and grammar. Reading through a revised draft multiple times can help you make sure you're correcting any errors. Use the checklist below to edit your sentences.

✔ Editing Checklist

- ☐ Are there any run-on sentences or sentence fragments to correct?
- ☐ Do all sentences have subject–verb agreement?
- ☐ Are quotations punctuated correctly with commas, quotation marks, and end punctuation placed appropriately?
- ☐ Are commas used correctly in compound and complex sentences?
- ☐ Are proper nouns—including names, acronyms, and titles—capitalized?
- ☐ Are all words spelled correctly?

Grammar Connections

Remember to place a comma after a word, phrase, or dependent clause that introduces a sentence. A comma is not needed if the dependent clause comes later in the sentence. Put a comma in front of the conjunction in a compound or a complex sentence.

Because it was getting late, I went to bed.

I went to bed because it was getting late.

It was getting late, and I went to bed.

List two mistakes you found as you proofread your research report.

1 _____

_____

2 _____

_____

Publish, Present, and Evaluate

Publishing When you **publish** your writing, you create a clean, neat final copy that is free of mistakes. Consider adding visuals, such as photographs, graphs, and tables that can help to support your argument.

Presentation When you are ready to **present** your work, rehearse your presentation. Use the Presenting Checklist to help you.

Evaluate After you publish your writing, use the rubric below to **evaluate** your writing.

What did you do successfully? _____

_____

What needs more work? _____

_____

✓ Presenting Checklist

- ☐ Convey confidence by making eye contact with your audience and speaking loudly and clearly.

- ☐ Use a friendly and upbeat tone of voice to engage your audience and share your opinion.

- ☐ Display any visuals prominently, and use natural gestures to draw the audience's attention to them.

- ☐ Expect questions from people with opposing views. Answer them respectfully.

4	3	2	1
• introduces the topic and states a claim in a clear and engaging way • develops support for the claim by presenting plenty of valid reasons and relevant evidence • effectively varies sentence structures to communicate ideas	• introduces the topic and states a claim • develops support by presenting several valid reasons and relevant evidence • varies some sentence structures to clearly communicate ideas	• identifies the topic but does not clarify a claim • supports ideas with a few reasons and some evidence that is not always valid or relevant • occasionally varies sentence structures; ideas are not always clear	• does not identify the topic or the claim • does not include valid reasons or relevant evidence • does not vary sentence structure; ideas are not clear

(h)Comstock Images/Alamy Stock Photo., (b)Andrea Paggiaro/Shutterstock. (bkgd)Andrey_Kuzmin/Shutterstock

Spiral Review

You have learned new skills and strategies in Unit 5 that will help you read more critically. Now it is time to practice what you have learned.

- **Make Inferences**
- **Cause and Effect**
- **Context Clues**
- **Letters**
- **Author's Point of View**

Connect to Content
- **Adages and Proverbs**
- **"Eye on the Sky"**

Read the selection and choose the best answer to each question.

Finding Our Way

1 In ancient times, people had to use their surroundings to <u>navigate</u>, otherwise they could get lost. Sea travelers hugged coastlines and noted important landmarks. Greek sailors used cloud formations to know when land was nearby. In the northern hemisphere, sailors could measure the distance from the North Star to the horizon to figure out where they were. The accuracy of these methods was limited, however. The invention of the compass allowed navigators to more accurately determine where and how they would arrive at their destination.

Early Discoveries

2 Many researchers say the compass has its beginnings in China about 2,000 years ago. They say historical records suggest a man named Luan Te made an accidental discovery. While setting up a board game, Luan Te found that one game piece, a rounded object with a long and thin handle, spun when placed on the board. When the game piece stopped spinning, its handle pointed in a north-south direction.

3 Luan Te's game piece likely pointed north and south because it contained lodestone, a common rock that acts as a natural magnet. Eventually, people began to understand that Earth's natural magnetic field affects magnetic objects. This knowledge would inspire people to create various devices that would ultimately lead to the invention of the compass we know today.

The south-pointer consisted of a spoon-shaped instrument made from lodestone placed on a bronze plate etched with symbols that represented planets and stars.

The Path to the Modern Compass

[4] Researchers say some time after Luan Te's discovery, the Chinese began to use a "south-pointer." This device was made by setting a spoon-shaped object of magnetized rock on a square base. Often, symbols representing stars and other natural objects were carved into the base. This device may have been used to help people avoid losing their way during travel.

[5] As time wore on, new devices that used Earth's magnetic field began to emerge. One such device was the wet compass. This consisted of a thin piece of iron, sometimes shaped like a fish, set in a bowl of water. The iron piece was rubbed against lodestone to make it magnetic. If set on a firm surface, the piece of iron was likely too heavy for it to be moved by Earth's magnetic field. But when placed in water, the iron piece would spin until it pointed north. The wet compass eventually became a valuable navigational aid.

[6] As navigational tools, these early compasses were far from perfect. They were not as precise as the compasses we use today because they did not indicate the range of directions other than due north and south. Eventually, people had the idea to pin a magnetized needle over a card. This was a dry compass. After marking the card to show north and south, the many directions between the two points could be drawn on the card. Now, navigators could feel more confident using the compass to explore unfamiliar lands and bodies of water.

[7] The modern compass uses the same basic technology as the early south-pointer. But today's compass needles are generally made of magnetized steel, and the compass is often set inside plastic. Of course, today's compasses are also much more reliable and precise.

While modern compasses like this one are more exact, they use the same basic design as did compasses from hundreds of years ago.

The Future

[8] Today, advanced technology helps us find our way. For example, the Global Positioning System allows GPS devices to use information from satellites in space to accurately pinpoint locations. But when accuracy is crucial, such as in mapmaking or during military exercises, the familiar compass is used to check the readings of a GPS device. And because a compass is not powered by electricity and does not rely on satellite signals, it can be used in the forests, deserts, oceans, and other locations that can pose problems to the reliability of a GPS device. For these reasons, the compass will continue to guide people across the land, seas, and skies for years to come.

Solomin Andrey/Shutterstock

SHOW WHAT YOU LEARNED

1 In paragraph 1, what words best help the reader know what <u>navigate</u> means?

  A In ancient times

  B people had to use

  C could get lost

  D sea travelers

2 Based on the information in paragraph 1, you can infer that —

  F Greek sailors did not use stars to navigate.

  G people did not travel over long distances.

  H it was risky to sail too far from the coast.

  J travelers had no way to know where they were headed.

3 In paragraph 3, the author uses a cause-and-effect text structure to help the reader understand —

  A why the Earth has a magnetic field

  B why Luan Te's game piece pointed in a north-south direction

  C who invented the modern compass

  D why Luan Te used lodestone in his game piece

4 The author's point of view that the compass will guide travelers for centuries to come is best supported by information about —

  F historic origins of the modern compass

  G high-tech devices like the GPS device

  H the materials used to make the modern compass

  J compasses that check GPS readings

> **Quick Tip**
>
> Eliminate any answer choices you know are wrong. Then use what you already know about the topic to infer a logical answer.

Read the selection and choose the best answer to each question.

CLAIRE'S JOURNEY

1 Claire O'Hara reread her father's letter for what felt like the hundredth time:

> July 22, 1907
>
> *My Dear Family,*
>
> *After four long years, I've finally arranged for your passage to America. With this letter are tickets for a steamship to New York. I shall meet you there, and we shall then travel to our home in Pennsylvania. You will love it as I do. I cannot wait to see you all.*
>
> *With love,*
>
> *Da*

2 Ten-year-old Claire thought her heart would leap from her chest. She was going to see Da again!

3 With as many of their belongings as they could stuff into suitcases, the family boarded the ship that would take them from Ireland to America. The ship set off. Claire, her mother, and her sister, Molly, saw the only land they'd known fade into the distance.

4 The 13-day voyage was <u>grueling</u>. The ship was crowded, the food poor, and the fresh water limited. Claire was tired and relieved when their ship finally pulled into New York Harbor. The ship's crew held back Claire's family, as well as a large number of other passengers, but allowed some people to leave the ship.

5 "Why can't we get off like those people?" Claire asked her mother.

ATLANTIC OCEAN

6   "They might be Americans returning from overseas. If you are immigrants, like us, you have to go to Ellis Island first."

7   The O'Haras waited for the short ferry ride from the ship to Ellis Island, a government immigration station. When they finally entered the Main Building at Ellis Island, all they could do was stare at the thousands of people. "How will Da ever find us?" Claire thought.

8   "Stay close together!" Ma said. Claire, holding tightly to Molly's hand, could barely hear Ma above the noise in the building's baggage room. It was overwhelming to have so many different people speaking so many different languages at once.

9   Men in uniforms took their bags and ushered the crowd of immigrants, including Claire, Ma, and Molly, up a giant staircase. There they met with a doctor. Claire noticed her mother wringing her hands. If the doctor found they had any illnesses, they could be held on the island or placed on a ship back home. Luckily, the three of them passed the examination.

10   The legal inspection came next. Molly squirmed against Claire as they waited in a long line until their ship number was called. After several hours, the O'Haras approached the inspectors' desks at the back of the Great Hall. A man checked their tags and spoke to Ma. He asked a lot of questions. Ma answered them all.

11   The inspector checked her responses against the information on the ship's manifest, or list of passengers aboard the ship. He seemed to be satisfied.

12   One official handed "landing cards" to Ma, Claire, and Molly. Relieved and excited, they made their way back downstairs and collected their bags. As they walked out of the building, they spotted him: There was Da, with his arms outstretched and his face beaming with joy!

1 Why is Da's letter in paragraph 1 important to the plot of "Claire's Journey"?

A   It tells the reader that Da can read and write.

B   It tells how and why Claire and her family will go to America.

C   It provides the names of all the characters in the story.

D   It explains what will happen at Ellis Island.

Quick Tip

If two answers seem correct, compare them. Then reread the question again to see which fits better.

2 In paragraph 4, <u>grueling</u> means —

F   very tiring

G   restful

H   exciting

J   short

3 In paragraph 9, what can you infer from Ma wringing her hands?

A   Ma is nervous about the doctor's examination.

B   Ma's hands hurt.

C   Ma is cold.

D   Ma is happy to be off the boat.

4 What is the effect of Claire, Ma, and Molly passing the doctor's examination and legal inspection?

F   They're made to return to Ireland.

G   Da is offered a job.

H   They're allowed entry into the United States.

J   They're allowed to the board the ship.

COMPARING GENRES

COLLABORATE

- In the **Literature Anthology,** reread the historical fiction text *Elijah of Buxton* on pages 350–365 and the folktale "The People Could Fly" on pages 368–371.

- Use the Venn diagram below to compare the texts. Remember that unlike characters in historical fiction, those in folktales do not need to behave as people do in real life. Think about these genre characteristics as you analyze how the selections are similar and different.

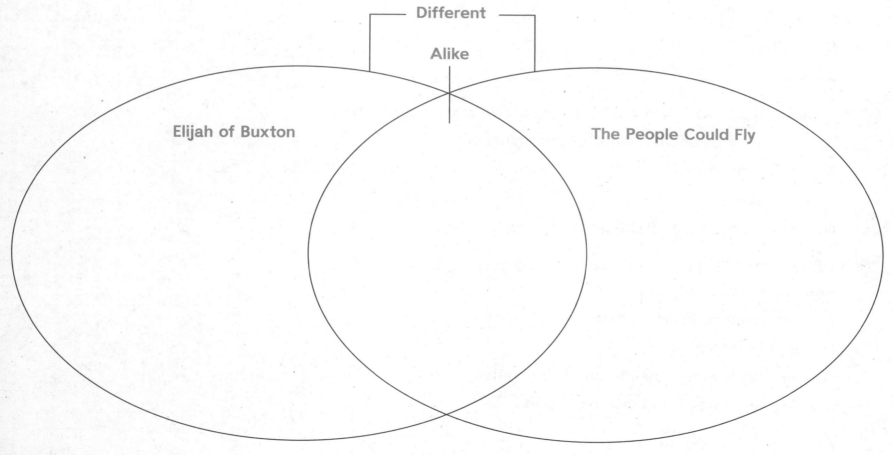

Different

Alike

Elijah of Buxton

The People Could Fly

CONTEXT CLUES: DEFINITIONS AND RESTATEMENTS

COLLABORATE

Authors often provide clues that point to the meaning of unfamiliar words. For example, an author may **restate** a difficult word using another term. An author may also provide a **definition** for a word in a nearby sentence. Restatements and definitions are usually set off with commas or dashes. Signal words and phrases such as *or, this means, that is,* or *in other words* also indicate a restatement or definition.

- Reread paragraph 1 of "The Science of Silk" on page 3. Notice the commas that signal a definition for *sericulture*: "Sericulture, the breeding of silkworms to produce silk, has improved greatly over the centuries."

- Use what you've learned to complete the chart. For each word, write the definition or restatement from "The Science of Silk" that helps you identify the word's meaning. Then write the meaning of the word.

Word/Page	Definition or Restatement from the Text	Meaning
larva, page 3		
Bombyx mori, page 3		
reeling, page 4		
throwing, page 4		
bobbins, page 4		

ADAGES AND PROVERBS

COLLABORATE

Abraham Lincoln, the sixteenth president of the United States, was a skilled orator known for such historic speeches as the Gettysburg Address. Lincoln often used adages and proverbs to express ideas in a humorous, yet thoughtful way. One of his famous sayings comes from a speech he gave before he became president: "A house divided against itself cannot stand." He used the adage to encourage unity as a way to reach success.

Research to find more adages and proverbs used by or attributed to Lincoln. Complete the chart with the adages and their meanings.

Adage or Proverb	Meaning

Think about some ideas you find interesting and create a few adages or proverbs to express them. Use those ideas to create your own booklet of adages or proverbs. Make sure to explain the meaning of each adage or proverb. Consider adding visuals related to your booklet.

C Squared Studios/Photodisc/Getty Images, (inset) Everett Historical/Shutterstock

EYE ON THE SKY

COLLABORATE

SCIENCE

Log on to **my.mheducation.com** and reread the *Time for Kids* online article "Eye on the Sky," including the information found in the interactive elements. Then answer the questions below.

Eye on the Sky

After out-of-this-world repairs, the Hubble Space Telescope makes us all eyewitnesses to the universe.

Time for Kids: "Eye on the Sky"

- Why was it important to make Hubble more sensitive to light?

_____

_____

- The author says that some people at NASA viewed Hubble as a "white elephant." Cite text evidence to explain whether or not the author agrees with this opinion.

_____

_____

_____

- What is the connection between Hubble and Galileo Galilei?

_____

_____

_____

- How does the "Meet an Astronaut" feature contribute to your understanding of the Hubble telescope?

_____

_____

_____

Purestock/SuperStock

TRACK YOUR PROGRESS

WHAT DID YOU LEARN?

Use the Rubric to evaluate yourself on the skills you learned in this unit.
Write your scores in the boxes below.

4	3	2	1
I can successfully identify all examples of this skill.	I can identify most examples of this skill.	I can identify a few examples of this skill.	I need to work more on this skill.

☐ Context Clues   ☐ Adages and Proverbs   ☐ Connotations and Denotations

☐ Cause and Effect   ☐ Author's Point of View

Something that I need to work more on is _____ because

_____

_____

_____

Text to Self Think back over the texts that you have read in this unit.
Choose one text and write a short paragraph explaining a personal
connection that you have made to the text.

I made a personal connection to _____ because _____

_____

_____

_____

_____.

Present Your Work

COLLABORATE

Discuss how you will present your timeline about the invention of space exploration tools. Use the Presenting Checklist as you practice your presentation. Discuss the sentence starters below and write your answers.

As I researched the history of tools used in space exploration, I discovered

_____

_____

_____

I would like to know more about _____

_____

_____

_____

NASA/Roscosmos

Talk About It

Essential Question

How have people used natural resources?

The beekeeper in this photo builds hives on his honey farm in Missouri. These hives provide safety for the bees' queen and a good environment for bees to manufacture their food supply. In return, the bees pollinate local crops, and the beekeeper is rewarded with a valuable commodity to sell: delicious honey.

More than ever, people are learning the importance of protecting such indispensable natural resources as bees. Talk to a partner about what comes to mind when you think of the importance of natural resources. Then write your ideas in the web.

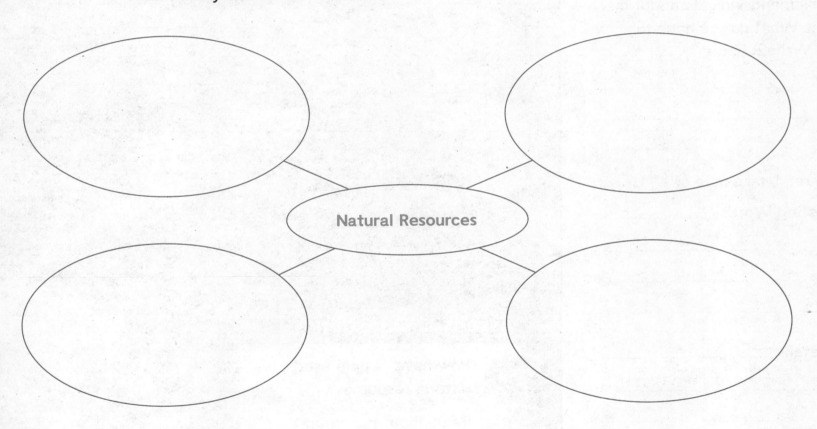

Natural Resources

Go online to **my.mheducation.com** and read the "A Valuable Resource" Blast. Think about what you know about natural resources and their uses. What are different ways people benefit from natural resources? Then blast back your response.

TAKE NOTES

You can set a purpose for reading by thinking about what you hope to learn from the text. First, scan the photos, captions, diagrams, and headings. Think about what these elements indicate about the content. What do you hope to learn? Write it here:

_____

_____

_____

As you read, take note of

Interesting Words _____

_____

_____

_____

Key Details _____

_____

_____

_____

_____

The Fortunes of Fragrance

Essential Question

?

How have people used natural resources?

Read about the natural resources used in the production of fragrances from ancient times to today.

Rose blossoms grown in the Atlas Mountains of Morocco

Hemis.fr/SuperStock

Our sense of smell plays a **significant** role in our survival. It helps us detect poisons, smoke from a fire, toxic gases, and other dangers. Our noses can tell us a great deal about something that is unfamiliar or questionable. For example, a piece of rotten fruit may look beautiful, but its smell lets us know it is not **edible.** For centuries, doctors have used their sense of smell to identify infection or disease. Fortunately, there are many pleasant odors as well. From earliest times, people have sought ways to preserve the lovely scents of flowers and herbs.

Capturing Aromas

Many plants contain volatile oils. These chemicals often repel insects, but they smell good to us. Early humans discovered them while crushing or bruising leaves, fruits, and bark. Before long, people found ways to release and use the oils. They noticed that soaking rose petals in water resulted in a scented liquid. They also learned that simply burning parts of aromatic plants would scent the air. People soon started to mix powdered resin, or tree sap, with honey to form lumps of incense. They placed the incense on hot coals or in **ornate** burners to produce a perfumed smoke. In fact, the word *perfume* comes from the Latin words *per* and *fumum,* meaning "through smoke."

Over time, people developed other means to capture fragrance from plants. They squeezed the rinds of citrus fruits or boiled the leaves of such plants as lavender and peppermint to obtain their oils. Later, they found that steam could extract oils from both fresh and dried plants. After the steam releases volatile oils from plant material inside a pressurized chamber, it passes through cooling tubes where the oils become a separate liquid. This technique of *steam distillation* is still widely used today.

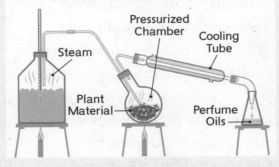

STEAM DISTILLATION

Steam

Pressurized Chamber

Cooling Tube

Plant Material

Perfume Oils

This diagram shows the steps in the process of steam distillation.

FIND TEXT EVIDENCE

Read

Paragraph 1

Main Idea and Key Details

What is the paragraph's main idea?

_____

_____

Underline text that supports this main idea.

Paragraphs 2–3 and Diagram

Logical Order

Draw a box around text that describes the process of steam distillation. How does the diagram support the text?

_____

_____

_____

Reread

Author's Craft

How does the author help you visualize how perfume is created?

SHARED READ

Read

Paragraph 1

Latin Roots

The root *solv* means "loosen." What do you think a *solvent* chemical does?

_____

_____

Paragraphs 2–3

Ask and Answer Questions

Write a question you can ask about trade routes and aromatics. Find and **underline** the answer.

_____

_____

_____

Reread

Author's Craft

Why do you think the author includes the photos and labels at the top of pages 102 and 103?

FLOWERS
Jasmine, Rose

PODS, SEEDS
Vanilla Pod, Anise Seed

BARK
Cinnamon, Birch

SAP, RESINS
Frankincense, Myrrh

CITRUS RINDS
Lime, Lemon

The petals of certain flowers cannot stand up to the heat of steam distillation, so people learned to press them gently into animal fat, which absorbs their fragrance. The fat is then washed in alcohol to draw out the fragrance molecules. After the alcohol evaporates, only the flower's fragrance remains as something called a *concrete*. This process, known as *enfleurage,* is both time-consuming and expensive. Today, solvent chemicals such as hexane are used to extract fragrance from delicate flowers.

Trading in Aromatics

Most fragrant plants are quite portable, so their **distribution** through vigorous trade was widespread throughout the ancient world. Depending on its availability, a treasured aromatic resource was often a more valuable **commodity** than gold or silver. Along Silk Road trade routes, Chinese merchants offered camphor for sale and purchased cinnamon and sandalwood from India. Egypt imported large quantities of myrrh. Caravans carried frankincense hundreds of miles by camel from Arabia to buyers in Greece and Rome. Eventually, Romans used so much incense that cargo ships were sent across the Mediterranean to speed up the way that supplies were **replenished**.

Trade in aromatics increased during the Middle Ages after people in Europe were introduced to the perfumes and spices of the Far East. But Europeans could buy these items only through merchants in the Middle East. Traders from that region had become the **dominant** players in the market and often charged extremely high prices. This monopoly on aromatic goods seemed **impenetrable**. So European explorers sought trade routes that went around the Middle East by sea.

BERRIES
Black Pepper,
Juniper Berry

WOOD
Sandalwood,
Cedar

LEAVES
Peppermint,
Patchouli

ROOTS, RHIZOMES
Vetiver Root,
Iris Rhizome

The Enduring Power of Perfume

In the modern world, trade involving fragrance materials is as brisk as ever. But chemists are the new explorers. Over several decades, these scientists have learned to isolate the fragrant molecules in natural plant oils and engineer synthetic replacements for others. Synthetic fragrance chemicals are derived primarily from petroleum. They are usually less expensive than natural materials, because supplies are not affected by weather conditions or crop yields.

Still, many of the highest-quality perfumes require a small percentage of ingredients derived from real flowers. One perfume company maintains its own fields in the south of France to grow the special kinds of rose and jasmine needed to produce

Hemis.fr/SuperStock

their best-selling product. Many companies use a process called *gas chromatography* to identify the molecules that make up a natural flower's fragrance. The molecules are then manufactured and blended to make a fragrance that simulates the real thing.

Demand for aromatics has only increased since ancient times. The production and sale of fragrance products make up an industry that is now worth billions of dollars. History has shown that, as long as people seek beautiful aromas, the fragrance market will continue to be big business.

Summarize

Use your notes to write a summary about this selection. Consider summarizing each section to write your summary.

FIND TEXT EVIDENCE

Read

Paragraphs 1–2

Ask and Answer Questions

Ask a question to check your understanding of the first two paragraphs. **Underline** the answer to your question.

_____

_____

_____

Paragraph 3

Main Idea and Key Details

Circle text that states the main idea of "The Enduring Power of Perfume."

Reread

Author's Craft

Why do you think the author titled this text "The Fortunes of Fragrance"?

Vocabulary

Use the example sentences to talk with a partner about each word. Then answer the questions.

commodity

Corn is an important **commodity** for farmers in the United States.

Name another commodity that is important for farmers.

_____

_____

distribution

The relief effort focused on **distribution** of medical supplies to flood victims.

Describe a time when you helped with the distribution of something.

_____

_____

dominant

The **dominant** wolf leads the pack of wolves.

How would you describe the behavior of a dominant person?

_____

_____

edible

All of the decorations on the cake were **edible**.

How are the meanings of the words _edible_ and _nutritious_ related?

_____

_____

impenetrable

Mario doubted that he would be able to get through the **impenetrable** crowd.

What else could you describe as impenetrable?

_____

_____

Build Your Word List Pick a word you found interesting in the selection you read. Look up synonyms and antonyms of the word in a print or digital thesaurus and write them in your writer's notebook.

ornate

I decorated my clay sculpture with an **ornate** design of curls.

What is an antonym of *ornate*?

_____

_____

_____

replenished

After I bought a bike, I **replenished** my savings by babysitting.

What is something else that must be replenished?

_____

_____

_____

significant

Eating more fruits and vegetables can have a **significant** effect on your health.

Describe something that has a significant effect on your ability to study.

_____

_____

_____

Latin Roots

You may not know the meaning of technical words in an expository text. Knowing common Latin roots can help you verify the meanings of unfamiliar words.

FIND TEXT EVIDENCE

In "The Fortunes of Fragrance" on page 101, I see the Latin root tract- *in the word* extract. *If I know that the Latin root* tract- *means "pull," I can use the word* from *as a context clue to figure out that* extract *means "pull from" or "remove."*

Later, they found that steam could <u>extract</u> oils from both fresh and dried plants.

Your Turn Use the Latin roots below and context clues to figure out the meaning of two words from "The Fortunes of Fragrance."

Latin roots: *port-* = "carry"   *sim-* = "make like"

portable, *page 102* _____

_____

simulates, *page 103* _____

_____

Ask and Answer Questions

When a passage in an expository text is unclear to you, ask yourself questions about it and then look for the answers as you read on. As you read "The Fortunes of Fragrance," pause frequently to consider what questions you have.

 FIND TEXT EVIDENCE

After reading the first paragraph of "Capturing Aromas" on page 101 of "The Fortunes of Fragrance," you may have had questions about what it means to "capture" aromas.

Page 101

Capturing Aromas

Many plants contain volatile oils. These chemicals often repel insects, but they smell good to us. Early humans discovered them while crushing or bruising leaves, fruits, and bark. Before long, people found ways to release and use the oils. They noticed that soaking rose petals in water resulted in a scented liquid. They also learned that simply burning parts of aromatic plants would scent the air.

I asked myself, "What is actually being captured and how?" I read that "plants contain volatile oils" and that people soaked or burnt plants to extract the oils. I'll look for more explanations as I read the rest of the section.

Your Turn What questions did you have after reading the first paragraph of "Trading in Aromatics" on page 102? Tell how you used details in the rest of the section to answer your questions.

_____

_____

_____

Logical Order

"The Fortunes of Fragrance" is an expository text that shares information about a topic. Like all good writing, an expository text presents details in a logical order, or an order that makes sense. Expository texts may contain diagrams to flesh out details in the main text.

🔍 FIND TEXT EVIDENCE

In "The Fortunes of Fragrance," the author uses a logical order to present facts about the use of plants for making fragrances. A diagram and other text features provide details that add to my understanding of the process of making perfume.

Page 101

Our sense of smell plays a **significant** role in our survival. It helps us detect poisons, smoke from a fire, toxic gases, and other dangers. Our noses can tell us a great deal about something that is unfamiliar or questionable. For example, a piece of rotten fruit may look beautiful, but its smell lets us know it is not **edible**. For centuries, doctors have used their sense of smell to identify infection or disease. Fortunately, there are many pleasant odors as well. From earliest times, people have sought ways to preserve the lovely scents of flowers and herbs.

Capturing Aromas

Many plants contain volatile oils. These chemicals often repel insects, but they smell good to us. Early humans discovered them while crushing or bruising leaves, fruits, and bark. Before long, people found ways to release and use the oils. They noticed that soaking rose petals in water resulted in a scented liquid. They also learned that simply burning parts of aromatic plants would scent the air. People soon started to mix powdered resin, or tree sap, with honey to form lumps of incense. They placed the incense on hot coals or in **ornate** burners to produce a perfumed smoke. In fact, the word *perfume* comes from the Latin words *per* and *fumum*, meaning "through smoke."

Over time, people developed other means to capture fragrance from plants. They squeezed the rinds of citrus fruits or boiled the leaves of such plants as lavender and peppermint to obtain their oils. Later, they found that steam could extract oils from both fresh and dried plants. After the steam releases volatile oils from plant material inside a pressurized chamber, it passes through cooling tubes where the oils become a separate liquid. This technique of *steam distillation* is still widely used today.

STEAM DISTILLATION

Steam
Pressurized Chamber
Cooling Tube
Plant Material
Perfume Oils

This diagram shows the steps in the process of steam distillation.

Logical Order

Steps in a process are explained in the order in which they happen.

Diagrams

Diagrams use visual images to explain and expand on concepts in the text.

COLLABORATE

Your Turn Reread paragraph 1 on page 102. Tell how the author uses logical order to describe the process of releasing fragrance from delicate flower petals.

_____

_____

_____

Main Idea and Key Details

The most important point an author makes about a topic is the main idea. When reading expository text, look for key details in each passage. Then think about what the details have in common to infer the main idea.

🔍 FIND TEXT EVIDENCE

When I reread "Capturing Aromas" on pages 101–102 of "The Fortunes of Fragrance," I can look for key details about the topic. To identify the main point the author is making, I can consider how all the details are related.

Main Idea
Ever since learning that plants contain fragrant chemicals, people have found ways to extract them.

↓

Detail
People discovered many plants that contain fragrant volatile oils.

↓

Detail
People soaked flowers and burned plants to release their fragrance.

↓

Detail
People used steam, animal fat, and chemical solvents to extract plant fragrances.

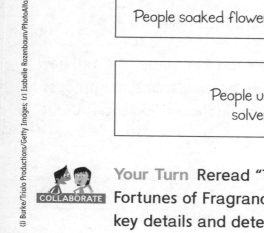 **Your Turn** Reread "Trading in Aromatics" on page 102 of "The Fortunes of Fragrance." Use the graphic organizer to identify key details and determine the main idea of the section.

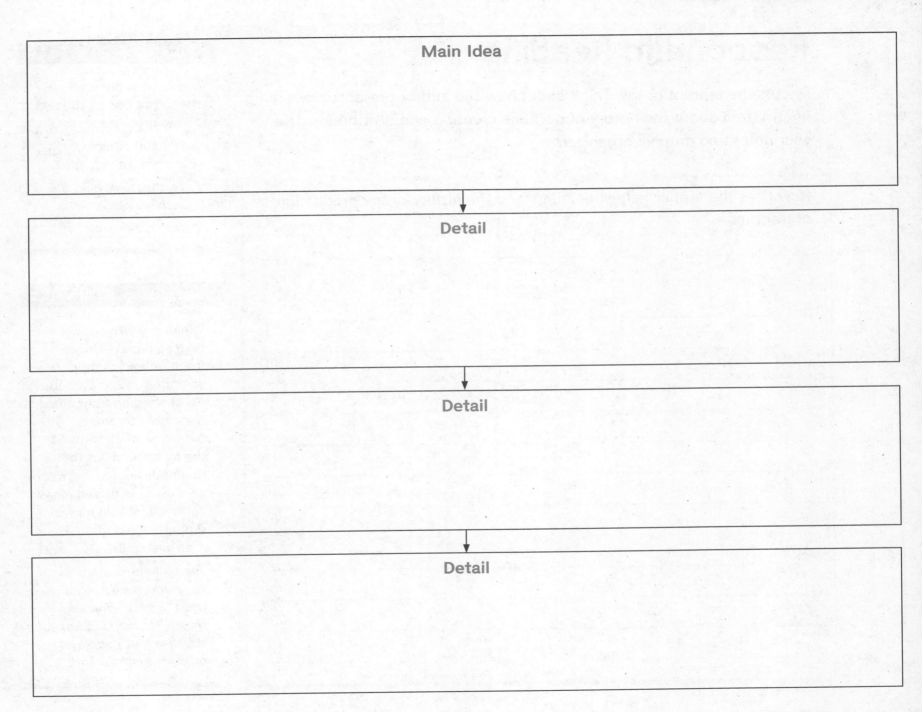

Main Idea

Detail

Detail

Detail

Respond to Reading

Discuss the prompt below. Think about how the author presents the information about the history of perfume creation and distribution. Use your notes and graphic organizer.

How does the author help you understand the history of the production of fragrances?

_____

_____

_____

_____

_____

_____

_____

_____

_____

_____

_____

_____

Quick Tip

Use these sentence starters to discuss the text and to organize ideas.

- *The author includes descriptive details to . . .*
- *Text features help the author . . .*
- *The author ends by . . .*

Readers to Writers

When you write about a text, you use evidence from the text to support your ideas. When you use exact wording from a text, remember to put quotation marks around the text. This helps the reader distinguish between your own words and ideas and the text evidence that supports these ideas. Here is an example:

The author uses sensory language, such as "hot coals" and "perfumed smoke," to help readers visualize how people produced early scents.

Photo Research

When you do **photo research**, you identify and compile relevant images to support your topic and ideas and to engage your audience. Although you can research photos in print materials, it's usually easiest to find suitable materials online. Think about the following questions as you conduct your photo research:

- Have I narrowed my search so I can quickly find good photos?
- Am I using reliable sources to find photos?
- Do the images give readers a better understanding of my ideas?

What other factors might impact your decision on whether to use a specific image you find?

_____

_____

Cranberries are our state's number one fruit crop. More cranberries are grown in Wisconsin than anywhere else in the nation! Juice from cranberries is a great source of vitamin C.

The photo and facts above give examples of a state product and its benefits.

COLLABORATE

Create a Collage With a partner or group, create a collage featuring photographs of products from your state. Include facts about each product and how it benefits people. Products can include natural resources, agricultural products, or manufactured products. Make sure to keep track of your sources. Consider these questions when researching products:

- What type of product is it? Why is it important to my state?
- What are some interesting facts about the product?
- How does the product benefit people?

Discuss the types of websites you might use for your research. After you finish, you will share your collage with your classmates.

Vilenia/Shutterstock

The Story of Salt

Literature Anthology:
pages 420–435

? How does the author use the sidebar to help you understand the main text?

 Talk About It Reread the sidebar on **Literature Anthology** page 422. Talk with a partner about what you learned about salt.

Cite Text Evidence What details help you understand more about salt? Write text evidence in the chart. Then write what the information helps you to understand.

 Evaluate Information

Authors often use sidebars to provide additional information about a specific topic covered in the text. Why might the author have considered the information in the sidebar on page 422 important?

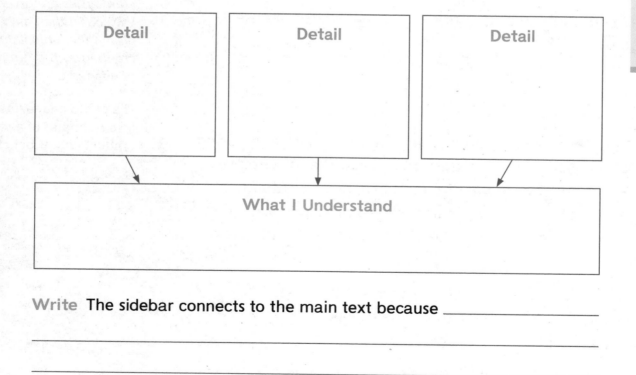

Detail	Detail	Detail

What I Understand

Write The sidebar connects to the main text because _____

_____

_____

_____

How does the author make it clear which type of text this is?

Talk About It Reread **Literature Anthology** pages 424-425. Talk with a partner about clues that show this text is expository.

Cite Text Evidence How do you know this is an expository text? Write text evidence in the chart.

Clue

↓

Clue

↓

Clue

Write The author makes it clear that this is an expository text by _____

_____

_____

_____

_____

? **How does the author use a timeline to help you understand the selection?**

Talk About It Reread the timeline on **Literature Anthology** pages 434 and 435. With a partner, talk about some important ideas in the timeline and how those ideas relate to the rest of the selection.

Cite Text Evidence What details from the timeline support an important idea you learned in *The Story of Salt?* Write text evidence in the chart.

Quick Tip

To read the timeline, start with the entry at the top of page 434 (9750 B.C.) and follow the ribbon that runs behind the text. Remember that more recent B.C. dates are represented by lower numbers. The numbers representing years begin to get larger once the A.D. time period starts.

What I Learned	Text Evidence

Write The timeline helps me understand the selection by _____

_____

_____

Alena Dvorakova/Yobi/123RF

Respond to Reading

COLLABORATE

Discuss the prompt below. Think about how the author was able to convey information about salt. Use your notes and graphic organizer.

How do the text features help you understand the rise and fall of salt?

The Not-So-Golden Touch

Literature Anthology:
pages 438–441

1   Long ago, a king named Midas ruled a large and peaceful kingdom. Midas loved to look at his paintings and his castle's fine furnishings, but most of all, he loved the large gold goblet and the golden statues that his staff polished every day. Midas knew he was a very lucky man to live surrounded by such beauty, but he also knew that the many golden objects in his possession made him a very rich man. Gold was a very rare and valuable commodity.

2   Midas was, however, not a terribly thoughtful man, and he tended to speak first and think later. One day Midas was riding in his carriage when he saw an old man sound asleep under a tree on the palace grounds. Midas was about to request that the trespasser be told to get off his property when one of Midas's minions spoke up, saying, "Surely we can let him sleep here, your highness. He is an old man, after all."

3   King Midas thought about it and agreed, saying, "Yes, let him sleep."

Reread the excerpt from the story. **Circle** the words that reveal King Midas's status.

Place a star next to text that describes a fault of the king's.

With a partner, **underline** the sentence that lets readers know the importance of gold as a resource. Talk about two different reasons that Midas loved gold. Write them here:

_____

_____

1   With that issue resolved, the king went to sleep happy, and the next morning he ordered a special breakfast. When it arrived, he picked up a silver fork, which immediately turned to gold. Then he took a bite of the steak and, following that, ate a forkful of egg, but somehow he felt disappointed. Something was missing, for this food didn't taste nearly as delicious as he remembered, and so the king immediately called for the cook.

2   Between Midas's outbursts, the cook tried patiently to explain that there was in fact something missing. Salt! Salt was now too valuable for anyone—even a king—to use as a seasoning on food.

3   The king sighed and picked at his bland food. He was beginning to realize what events he had set in motion and how, because of his greed, his food would never taste the same again.

Reread the excerpt from the story. **Circle** details that tell you the king thinks he has solved all of his problems. Write the two problems the king still has here:

1. _____

2. _____

Talk with a partner about why it's a problem that Midas and the ministers have chosen to replace gold with salt as currency. **Underline** why the king can no longer put salt on his food.

How does the author show the importance of thinking ahead?

Talk About It Look back at the excerpts on pages 116 and 117. Talk with a partner about the mistakes Midas makes in the story.

Cite Text Evidence What are the consequences of King Midas's actions? Write text evidence in the chart.

Synthesize Information

Thinking about the consequences of a character's actions can often lead you to discover a story's theme, or important message. Once you've identified the consequences, consider what the character has learned from his or her experiences. Then determine how this might reflect a message the author wants readers to understand.

Action	Consequence

Write The author shows thinking ahead is important by _____

_____

_____

_____

Figurative Language

Authors use **figurative language**, such as similes, metaphors, and personification, to help readers visualize and gain a deeper understanding of important ideas and events. Similes compare items using the word *like* or *as*. Metaphors compare items without using those words. Personification gives human qualities to non-human objects, animals, or ideas.

 FIND TEXT EVIDENCE

In paragraph 4 of "The Not-So-Golden Touch" on **Literature Anthology** page 440, the author uses the simile "as common as dirt" to convey the idea that gold is no longer special.

> "Gold was valuable only when it was rare, but you have turned so many things into gold that it's now everywhere and it's as common as . . . as dirt!" said the minister.

COLLABORATE

Your Turn Reread paragraph 5 on Literature Anthology page 440.

- Describe how the author uses figurative language in the paragraph.

  _____

  _____

- How does this use of figurative language help readers create a mental image?

  _____

  _____

Text Connections

? **How do the illustrator's use of details and the authors' use of text features in *The Story of Salt* and "The Not-So-Golden Touch" help you understand the importance of natural resources?**

Quick Tip

The people in the illustration are merchants. Talk about what you think they are transporting. Why might they be transporting these things?

Talk About It Look at the illustration. Describe to a partner what you see and how you know what the people are doing is important.

Cite Text Evidence **Circle** clues in the illustration that show things are being transported. **Underline** information in the caption that gives more detail about what is happening in the illustration.

Write The details in the illustration and text features in the selections

help me to _____

_____

_____

_____

_____

_____

This illustration of a 13th century camel caravan shows merchants, camels, and horses.

Peter Dennis/Getty Images

SCIENCE

Present Your Work

COLLABORATE

Discuss how you will present your photo collage of products from your state. Be prepared to list the sources you used in your research. Use the Presenting Checklist as you practice your presentation. Discuss the sentence starters below and write your answers.

Presenting Checklist

☐ Plan with your group how you will present your collage.

☐ Think about some questions your audience may have and be prepared to answer them.

☐ Rehearse your presentation with your group.

☐ Speak clearly, enunciating every word.

After researching products from our state, I learned _____

_____

_____

I am interested in finding out more about _____

_____

_____

SpeedKingz/Shutterstock

Literature Anthology: pages 420–435

Expert Model

Features of a Research Report

A research report is an expository text that informs readers about a topic based on relevant information gathered from a variety of reliable sources. A research report

- introduces topics and ideas in a clear manner;

- develops a topic with facts, specific details, and examples gathered from research;

- organizes information in a logical order.

Analyze an Expert Model Studying expository texts will help you learn how to plan and write a research report. **Reread** the section "How to Make Salt" on page 423 of *The Story of Salt* in the **Literature Anthology.** Then answer the questions below.

How does the first paragraph of this section introduce its topic in a way that helps you determine your purpose for reading the section? _____

_____

_____

What relevant information helps you understand where humans first found salt? _____

_____

_____

Readers to Writers

On page 423, the author has included an illustration to show what a dry salt bed looks like. Research reports sometimes include text features, such as diagrams, illustrations, charts, and photographs, to give clarifying, supporting, or additional information. As you plan your report, think about what text features you might want to include.

Plan: Choose Your Topic

Brainstorm A spice is a plant root, seed, or fruit used for flavoring. Examples are cinnamon, pepper, and nutmeg. With a partner, brainstorm a list of spices you've tasted or would like to try someday. Write your ideas below.

_____

_____

_____

Writing Prompt Choose a spice from your list and write a research report that answers these questions: What is the history of the spice? Is it used in food and beverages today? Include scientific information about the spice as part of your report. For example, you might help readers understand how a spice is cultivated and processed.

I will research and write about _____

Purpose and Audience Think about who will read your report. Will your purpose be to inform, persuade, or entertain?

My purpose for writing is to _____

Plan In your writer's notebook, make a Topic/Example/Detail web to plan your writing. Fill in the Topic section with the spice you have chosen. Complete the other sections as you research. You may need to add more sections to fully cover your topic.

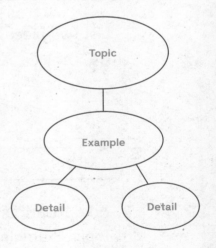

Plan: Relevant Information

Choose Relevant Information Relevant information is information directly connected to the topic you are researching. To help you focus on the information you need, write down specific questions about your chosen spice that you want your research to answer. As you review sources, also consider these questions:

• Does this source contain facts, details, and examples about my topic?

• Is the information current, accurate, and written by an expert?

• Have I used a variety of sources in order to find different kinds of information?

List two pieces of relevant information for your research report.

1 _____

_____

2 _____

_____

Take Notes Once you have chosen your sources, take notes and fill in your Topic/Example/Detail graphic organizer. Keep track of your sources in case you need to refer to them again and for when you cite them.

Digital Tools

For more information about planning and organizing a research report, watch "How to Create an Outline." Go to **my.mheducation.com**.

Draft

Domain-Specific Vocabulary Writers of research reports use domain words, or words specific to their subject, to help readers better understand information. In the example below from "The Fortunes of Fragrance," the writer uses scientific domain words such as *molecule* and *synthetic* to help readers understand part of the process of making fragrances.

> Over several decades, these scientists have learned to isolate the fragrant molecules in natural plant oils and engineer synthetic replacements for others. Synthetic fragrance chemicals are derived primarily from petroleum.

Now use the paragraph as a model to write information about the spice you chose for your topic. Make sure to include appropriate domain words.

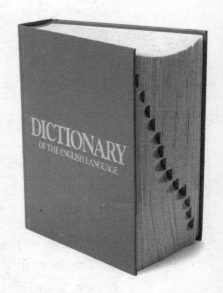

_____

_____

_____

_____

Write a Draft Use your Topic/Example/Detail graphic organizer to help you write your draft in your writer's notebook. Include the most relevant information you collected from credible sources.

Revise

Logical Order When you revise a draft, check that your facts and details are presented in a logical order. Readers should be able to follow the ideas and understand their connection. Read the sample paragraph below. Then revise it so that the facts and details are in the most logical order.

> Cinnamon is the inner bark of cinnamon trees. But where does it come from? When this bark is harvested and dried, it curls into rolls, or quills. Both cinnamon sticks and cinnamon powder are made from these quills. Cinnamon is a very popular spice.

Quick Tip

Not all paragraphs in a research report have to be organized the same way. Some may be organized to show a sequence of events or steps in a process. Others may show a cause and an effect, or a problem and a solution. Choose the logical order that makes the most sense for the information you are presenting.

_____

_____

_____

_____

_____

Revision As you revise your draft, check that you present your facts and details in a logical order. Think about what will most help your readers understand the information. Make sure your information correctly tells what you found in your research.

Peer Conferences

Review a Draft Listen carefully as a partner reads his or her work aloud. Take notes about what you liked and what was difficult to follow. Begin by telling what you liked about the draft. Ask questions that will help the writer think more about the writing. Make suggestions that you think will make the writing stronger. Use these sentence starters.

I enjoyed this part of your draft because . . .

Can you clarify the connection between . . . and your topic?

Think about adding a domain-specific word, such as . . .

Reordering the details in this paragraph would help you . . .

Partner Feedback After your partner gives you feedback on your draft, write one of the suggestions that you will use in your revision. Refer to the rubric on page 129 as you give feedback.

Based on my partner's feedback, I will _____

_____

_____

After you finish giving each other feedback, reflect on the peer conference. What was helpful? What might you do differently next time?

Revision As you revise your draft, use the Revising Checklist to help you figure out what text you may need to move, elaborate on, or delete. Remember to use the rubric on page 129 to help you with your revision.

✔ Revising Checklist

☐ Does my writing fit my purpose and audience?

☐ Have I included information that is relevant to my topic and based on credible sources?

☐ Have I organized my information in a logical order?

☐ Did I include domain-specific vocabulary to tell about my topic?

WRITING

Edit and Proofread

When you **edit** and **proofread** your writing, you look for and correct mistakes in spelling, punctuation, capitalization, and grammar. Reading through a revised draft multiple times can help you make sure you're correcting any errors. Use the checklist below to edit your sentences.

✓ Editing Checklist

- ☐ Do all sentences have subject–verb and pronoun–antecedent agreement?
- ☐ Are domain-specific words used in the proper scientific context?
- ☐ Are commas correctly used to separate items in a series?
- ☐ Are all proper nouns and titles capitalized?
- ☐ Are all quotations properly punctuated?
- ☐ Are book titles underlined or italicized?
- ☐ Are all words spelled correctly?

List two mistakes you found as you proofread your research report.

1 _____

_____

2 _____

_____

Grammar Connections

When you proofread, make sure the subjects and verbs in your sentences agree. The simple subject is the principal word or words in the subject. Make the action verb or linking verb agree in number with the subject. For example: *Ginger has a spicy flavor. Ginger roots are often peeled before cooking.*

VGstockstudio/Shutterstock

Publish, Present, and Evaluate

Publishing When you **publish** your writing, you create a clean, neat final copy that is free of mistakes. Be sure to write neatly. Consider adding headings and graphics such as photos, tables, and charts to help readers understand the information in your research report.

Presentation When you are ready to **present** your work, rehearse your presentation. Use the Presenting Checklist to help you.

Evaluate After you publish your writing, use the rubric below to **evaluate** your writing.

What did you do successfully? _____

What needs more work? _____

_____

Presenting Checklist

- ☐ Practice saying any difficult domain-specific words aloud.
- ☐ Speak clearly, slowly, and loudly enough for all to hear.
- ☐ Make regular and sustained eye contact with your audience.
- ☐ Listen actively and respond to questions thoughtfully, using details from your topic.

4	3	2	1
• presents relevant facts from credible sources to discuss a clearly stated topic • correctly uses domain-specific vocabulary related to the topic • consistently organizes the information in a logical order	• presents relevant facts from credible sources to discuss a topic • uses some domain-specific vocabulary related to the topic • presents information in a mostly logical order	• presents some relevant facts from mostly credible sources to discuss a topic • uses little correct domain-specific vocabulary related to the topic • makes an effort to present information in a logical order	• presents few, if any, facts about the topic; no credible sources were consulted • doesn't use domain-specific vocabulary • does not present information in a logical order

Imagine unearthing thousands of soldiers made of fired clay, all lined up in trenches underground. That's exactly what happened in China's Shaanxi Province in 1974. This army of life-sized terra-cotta soldiers was created with meticulous care more than 2,000 years ago to protect the tomb of China's first emperor. Amazingly, no two soldiers are identical. Each statue has distinct facial features, and many carry very real—and very sharp—weapons.

Talk with a partner about what you see in the photograph. Discuss what we can learn from discovering objects from the past. Write your ideas in the web below.

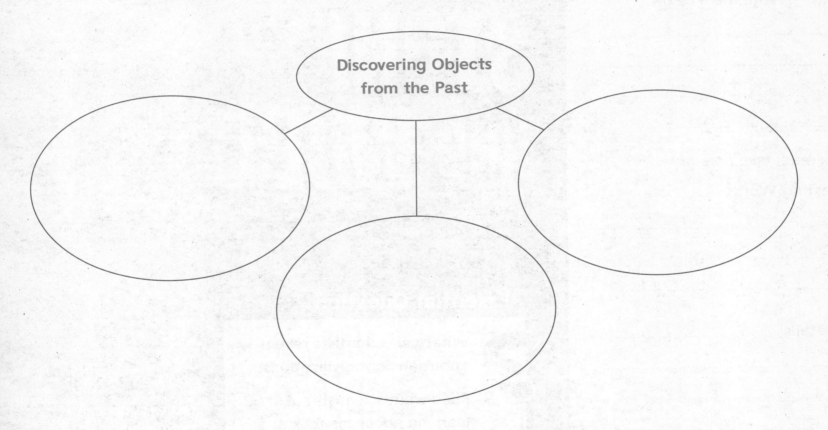

Discovering Objects from the Past

Go online to **my.mheducation.com** and read the "You Are What You Eat" Blast. Think about the kinds of food people commonly eat today. What might researchers in the future learn from studying our diet today? Then blast back your response.

TAKE NOTES

Asking questions before you read and then looking for answers helps you gain information. Before you read, look at the title, headings, and images. What questions do you have? Write them below.

_____

_____

_____

_____

As you read, take note of

Interesting Words _____

_____

_____

_____

Key Details _____

_____

_____

_____

_____

_____

_____

MESSAGES IN STONE AND WOOD

Essential Question

What can scientists reveal about ancient civilizations?

Read what scientists are learning about the rock and tree art of Native Americans.

Native American petroglyphs, Canyon de Chelly, Arizona

Pete Ryan/National Geographic/Getty Images

"We Were Here"

Deep in a forest in what is now Pennsylvania, members of a hunting party were preparing to **embark** on their trip home. Only one task remained: creating a chronicle of their successful hunt. One of the hunters selected a broad oak tree, carefully made some cuts with his knife, and used the blade to peel back the bark. From a small leather bag, he shook out some powder he had ground from red pebbles. Then he mixed the powder with animal fat to make a thick red paint.

On the tree, the hunter **meticulously** painted images of a turtle and six men carrying packs and bows. Next, he drew a circle, a half circle, and six marks. Finally, he added the heads of three deer and a bear. From then on, anyone passing this spot would see from these designs that six men of the terrapin clan had hunted here. They had camped for one and a half moons, plus six days. And they had had a successful hunt.

Mysterious Markings

The first Europeans to explore North America came across many markings like the ones on that Pennsylvania tree. At first, no one understood the meanings of these mysterious *petroglyphs* (stone carvings) and *dendroglyphs* (tree carvings and paintings). Nor did they know who had created them. As time went on, however, people studying the markings, or pictographs, began to understand that they had been made by Native Americans. They concluded that the pictographs were records of hunts, battles, and clan meetings. They seemed also to serve as directions, warnings, boundary markers, and clan identifications.

Petroglyph of a "Water Panther," Parkers Landing, Pennsylvania

Photo by Paul Nevin/Courtesy of the State Museum of Pennsylvania, Pennsylvania Historical and Museum Commission

FIND TEXT EVIDENCE

Read

Paragraphs 1–2

Sequence

Circle words that tell you the order of the hunter's actions. What was the result of the hunter's actions?

_____

_____

Paragraph 3

Summarize

Underline key details in paragraph 3. Then summarize the paragraph.

_____

_____

_____

_____

_____

Reread

Author's Craft

How is "We Were Here" unlike the other sections? Why might the author present the text this way?

SHARED READ

FIND TEXT EVIDENCE

Read

Lists

What is something you learn from the list of petroglyph types?

_____

_____

Paragraph 1
Make Inferences

What can you infer about how direct sunlight affects the carvings?

_____

_____

Paragraphs 2–3
Sequence

Underline evidence that tells how archaeologists figured out how to determine the age of markings.

Reread

Author's Craft

How does the author structure the text to show how researchers have learned more about pictographs?

COMMON PETROGLYPH TYPES

 human figures

dog

hand

fish

spiral

half moon

bird

sheep

elk or deer

snake

When non-native people pushed farther west during the 1800s, they discovered many more of these images. In the dry desert of the Southwest, **exquisite** pictographs on rocks and cave walls appeared to be freshly made. This was especially true of carvings protected from direct sunlight. In the East, however, moisture decomposes dead tree trunks and winter ice damages rocks. Pictographs generally survive this wetter and colder climate only in sheltered spots. These spots are often outcroppings of **bedrock** that have been covered over by soil or moss. As a result, the only remaining records of many vanished pictographs are copies that were sketched by early explorers and historians.

Reading the Messages

For a long time, archaeologists made little progress in studying the rock art of Native Americans. They could not reliably date the pictographs, relate them to other human artifacts, or even agree on their meanings. But as technology improved, scientists learned much more about these **intriguing** images. For example, they used radiocarbon dating to measure the decay rate of carbon in the paint of dendroglyphs. By analyzing how rock surfaces had weathered, they estimated that some petroglyphs were nearly a thousand years old.

Although dating is now more reliable, understanding the meanings of rock images remains difficult. It is generally accepted that the people who made pictographs in open areas wanted to mark borders or record significant events. But interpreting images hidden in sheltered areas or caves has been more challenging.

Archaeologist Rex Weeks, an Echota Cherokee from Alabama, has brought an **intrinsic** cultural perspective to the scientific study and interpretation of Native American rock images. Dr. Weeks suggests that petroglyphs in secluded locations were purposely made at sites that would not be accessible to outsiders. The images were intended primarily for ceremonial use. Elders may also have used them to teach young people the beliefs and history of their clan. Weeks's research has shown that many of the symbols employed in pictographs link the cultures of ancient peoples to existing oral traditions of Native Americans. And by conducting experiments with hammer and chisel stones, Weeks has been able to demonstrate his theories about the techniques used to create rock carvings.

Preserving the Past

Today, many pictographs are in danger of being destroyed by natural forces before they can be documented and studied. Others are damaged when careless **excavation** by non-professionals defaces them or leaves them exposed to the elements. So experts have developed a system called the Rock Art Stability Index to assess in a **methodical** way which sites are most at risk. They also enlist trained volunteers, including Native people, to record and manage newly discovered sites. One such site, a cave in the Appalachian Mountains, contains fragile rock art that is more than a thousand years old. Educating the public about the importance and vulnerability of these sites is critical if the efforts of archaeologists such as Dr. Weeks are to succeed in preserving these rich cultural resources for future generations.

Summarize

Use your notes to orally summarize what scientists have learned about ancient Native American pictographs and what they still want to know.

FIND TEXT EVIDENCE 🔍

Read

Paragraph 1
Greek Roots

The Greek root *techn-* means "skill or art." What are *techniques*?

_____

_____

Paragraph 2
Summarize

Underline key details in "Preserving the Past." Summarize the section.

_____

_____

_____

_____

_____

_____

Reread

Author's Craft

Why is "Preserving the Past" a good heading for this section?

Vocabulary

Use the example sentences to talk with a partner about each word. Then answer the questions.

bedrock

The construction crew dug out the soil until they hit **bedrock**.

How would you know if you hit bedrock?

_____

_____

embark

Once we have put our luggage in the car, we can **embark** on our vacation.

How are the meanings of *embark* and *start* related?

_____

_____

excavation

To learn more about the ancient town, archaeologists began an **excavation**.

What might archaeologists find during an excavation?

_____

_____

exquisite

The queen's jewelry was **exquisite**.

What else could be described as exquisite?

_____

_____

intriguing

The astronomer thought the idea of life on distant planets was **intriguing**.

What is something you find intriguing?

_____

_____

 Build Your Word List Reread page 133. Circle a word you found interesting. In your writer's notebook, make a word web with the word you chose in the center. Add forms of the word to the web. Repeat for pages 134 and 135.

intrinsic

A school is an **intrinsic** part of a community.

What is another intrinsic part of a community?

_____

_____

_____

methodical

The student's **methodical** preparation ensured she was ready for the test.

What is something that works best when it's done in a methodical way?

_____

_____

_____

meticulously

Leon **meticulously** painted each detail on the model.

What is another word that means about the same thing as *meticulously*?

_____

_____

Greek Roots

Scientific words in expository texts often contain Greek roots. Knowing the meanings of Greek roots can help you figure out the meanings of unfamiliar words in context. Some common Greek roots include *chron-* ("time"), *gen-* ("birth"), and *-graph* ("written").

🔍 FIND TEXT EVIDENCE

I see the word archaeologists *on page 134 of* "Messages in Stone and Wood." *The Greek root* archaeo- *means "ancient" or "original," and I can use the context clue "studying" to figure out that* archaeologists *are people who study ancient objects.*

For a long time, archaeologists made little progress in studying the rock art of Native Americans.

Your Turn Use the Greek roots above and context clues to define these words from "Messages in Stone and Wood."

chronicle, *page 133* _____

pictographs, *page 133* _____

generations, *page 135* _____

Pete Ryan/National Geographic/Getty Images

Summarize

To summarize information in an expository text, use your own words to restate important ideas and details. Be sure to not express your opinions.

Quick Tip

A summary does not include everything from a text. Only include the most important information.

🔍 FIND TEXT EVIDENCE

You may not be sure of the author's most important points in the second paragraph of "Mysterious Markings." Reread the paragraph on page 134.

> Page 134
>
> In the dry desert of the Southwest, **exquisite** pictographs on rocks and cave walls appeared to be freshly made. This was especially true of carvings protected from direct sunlight. In the East, however, moisture decomposes dead tree trunks and winter ice damages rocks. Pictographs generally survive this wetter and colder climate only in sheltered spots. These spots are often outcroppings of **bedrock** that have been covered over by soil or moss. As a result, the only remaining records of many vanished pictographs are copies that were sketched by early explorers and historians.

I read that pictographs in the Southwest looked new, while most of those in the East were aged by water and ice. I can summarize by saying climate and weather affect the lifespan of pictographs.

Your Turn Summarize the first paragraph of "Reading the Messages" on page 134.

_____

_____

_____

Photographs and Lists

The selection "Messages in Stone and Wood" is an expository text. An expository text presents information and facts about a topic in a logical order. It may include photographs for visual support and lists to display or catalogue items in an organized way.

🔍 FIND TEXT EVIDENCE

"Messages in Stone and Wood" explains what the pictographs of early Native Americans are and how people have studied them over many years. Photographs provide visual support for the information, and a labeled list shows illustrations of representative items in an easy-to-understand way.

Page 134

When non-native people pushed farther west during the 1800s, they discovered many more of these images. In the dry desert of the Southwest, **exquisite** pictographs on rocks and cave walls appeared to be freshly made. This was especially true of carvings protected from direct sunlight. In the East, however, moisture decomposes dead tree trunks and winter ice damages rocks. Pictographs generally survive this wetter and colder climate only in sheltered spots. These spots are often outcroppings of **bedrock** that have been covered over by soil or moss. As a result, the only remaining records of many vanished pictographs are copies that were sketched by early explorers and historians.

Reading the Messages

For a long time, archaeologists made little progress in studying the rock art of Native Americans. They could not reliably date the pictographs, relate them to other human artifacts, or even agree on their meanings. But as technology improved, scientists learned much more about these **intriguing** images. For example, they used radiocarbon dating to measure the decay rate of carbon in the paint of dendroglyphs. By analyzing how rock surfaces had weathered, they estimated that some petroglyphs were nearly a thousand years old.

Although dating is now more reliable, understanding the meanings of rock images remains difficult. It is generally accepted that the people who made pictographs in open areas wanted to mark borders or record significant events. But interpreting images hidden in sheltered areas or caves has been more challenging.

Readers to Writers

Lists often allow writers of expository texts to include additional facts, examples, or details that they don't have space to include in the main text. When you write your own expository text, consider if using a list would be an effective way of providing additional relevant information about your topic.

Photographs

Photographic images provide visual documentary evidence.

Lists

Lists organize and display a series of items in a logical way.

Your Turn Explain how the photographs on pages 132–133 and the list on page 134 add to your understanding of the text.

_____

_____

_____

_____

_____

_____

Sequence

Authors of expository texts organize facts and information in a logical way. They frequently use a chronological, or time-order, sequence to explain when and why things happened.

🔍 **FIND TEXT EVIDENCE**

When I reread the first two sections of "Messages in Stone and Wood," I can look for details about when events occurred. The section "We Were Here" does not state when the hunters lived. When I reread "Mysterious Markings," I conclude that they lived before "the first Europeans to explore North America" arrived.

> **Event**
> Early Native Americans left pictographs describing their successful hunt.

↓

> Europeans arriving in North America wanted to know the meanings of the mysterious markings they saw.

↓

>

↓

>

Your Turn Reread the rest of "Messages in Stone and Wood." Identify additional key events in time-order sequence. List the events in the graphic organizer.

Event

Early Native Americans left pictographs describing their successful hunt.

↓

Europeans arriving in North America wanted to know the meanings of the mysterious markings they saw.

↓

↓

↓

Respond to Reading

COLLABORATE Discuss the prompt below. Think about how the author presents the information. Use your notes and graphic organizer.

How does the author help readers understand how knowledge of Native American pictographs has grown over time?

_____

_____

_____

_____

_____

_____

_____

_____

_____

_____

_____

_____

_____

_____

Relevant Information

When researching a topic, look for information that is relevant, or connected to your topic. Thoughtful research questions can help you focus your search for relevant information. As you research a topic, ask yourself:

- Does this information answer my research questions?
- Does this information directly support my main points?
- Will this information help my audience better understand the topic?

How might you begin a search for relevant information?

_____

_____

_____

- Many people come to view the petroglyphs in Utah.
- This petroglyph, found in Utah, was created by people of the Fremont culture.

A student found the facts above while researching how petroglyphs helped people communicate. Which fact is more relevant to her topic? Explain your reasoning.

_____

_____

_____

_____

_____

_____

_____

_____

Illustrate a Book With a partner or group, research other petroglyphs found throughout history. Then create a book displaying images you find. Explain the meanings of the images and describe where they came from. Consider these questions when looking for relevant information:

- Who created this petroglyph?
- Where was the image found? What does its location tell you about its purpose or creators?
- What message might the image have been meant to communicate?

Discuss how you will illustrate your book. Will you draw the petroglyphs or use printouts or digital images? When you are finished, you will share your book with your classmates.

Pharaoh's Boat

Literature Anthology: pages 442–457

? **How does the author use an illustrated list to support the text?**

COLLABORATE

Talk About It Reread **Literature Anthology** page 447 and review the list of tools. Talk with a partner about why the author includes illustrations.

Cite Text Evidence What details in the text on page 447 help you understand some of the uses for the tools? Write them in the web.

 Evaluate Information

Authors must make decisions about how to best present different kinds of information. Why do you think the author chose a list to convey information about the different kinds of woodworking tools? Do you think this is an effective presentation of the information? Explain why or why not.

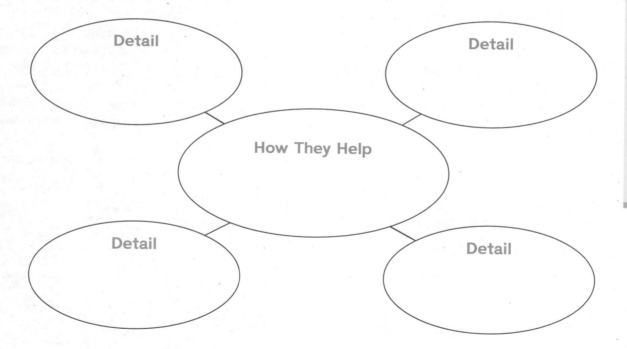

Detail

Detail

How They Help

Detail

Detail

Write The author uses the list to help me understand _____

_____

_____

_____

How does the author help you understand Mallakh's feeling of history?

Talk About It Reread the second paragraph on **Literature Anthology** page 451. Discuss with a partner the sensory language Mallakh uses.

Cite Text Evidence What does Mallakh conclude from what he sees and smells in the chamber? Record text evidence and his conclusion below.

Clues	Conclusion

Write The author helps me understand Mallakh's feeling of history by _____

_____

_____

_____

Quick Tip

Authors use sensory language to appeal to a reader's five senses. As you read the text, look for language that provides vivid descriptions of how something looked, smelled, or sounded.

Make Inferences

The author says Mallakh smelled cedar "as fragrant as if it had been placed there the year before." What does this description tell you about the condition of the boat and about how effective the ancient Egyptians' preservation techniques were?

? How does the author help you understand Ahmed's struggle to rebuild the ancient ship?

Talk About It Reread **Literature Anthology** pages 454–455. Talk with a partner about why it's difficult to reconstruct an ancient ship.

Cite Text Evidence What problems does Ahmed face, and how is he able to solve the problems? Record problems and their solutions in the chart.

Problem	Solution

Write The author helps me understand Ahmed's struggle by _____

_____

_____

Lisa S./Shutterstock

Synthesize Information

On page 453, Ahmed says that putting the boat together was "like trying to complete a jigsaw puzzle without having the picture on the box." How do the problems and solutions Ahmed faced help you understand this statement?

Respond to Reading

Discuss the prompt below. Think about the role and importance of a pharaoh in ancient Egyptian life. Use your notes and graphic organizer.

Why does the author include the history of pharaohs and their importance to Egyptian culture?

_____

_____

_____

_____

_____

_____

_____

_____

_____

_____

_____

_____

Quick Tip

Use these sentence starters to talk about and cite text evidence.

- *The illustrations and captions help me to . . .*
- *The author uses historical details to . . .*
- *This helps me understand that . . .*

Self-Selected Reading

Connecting what you read to what you already know helps you learn. Choose a text, and write its title, author, and genre in your writer's notebook. As you read, make connections to personal experiences, to what you already know, and to other texts you've read. Write your ideas in your notebook.

The Mystery of the Missing Sandals

Literature Anthology:
pages 460-463

1   Starting in June, the museum had started getting pretty crowded because it had a traveling exhibit on King Tutankhamun. That's King Tut to you. The exhibit is filled with incredible artifacts, even an alabaster jar with a sculpture of the king on top that once held King Tut's mummified stomach. In case you don't know, Tut was sort of a minor king, but the ancient Egyptians still buried him in style in a tomb archaeologist Howard Carter unearthed in 1922.

Reread the excerpted paragraph from "The Mystery of the Missing Sandals." **Underline** details in the paragraph that a reader could research to verify as true, historical facts.

COLLABORATE

Discuss with a partner the details of the excerpt that you would not be able to verify as true. Which details are likely made up to develop the plot of the story?

_____

_____

_____

_____

_____

_____

1 "Oh, hi Scott," Alice answered as she looked up. "It's one of several boats in the collection from King Tut's tomb, and I'm just giving it a final inspection for the exhibit. This is the smallest one. And I've uncovered this amazing detail—see this extra hole on the deck? I'm guessing there might have been another mast on this boat that was broken off long ago."

2 "Why were there so many boats found in the tomb?" I wondered aloud. "Wasn't Tutankhamun buried in the desert?"

3 "Boats were extremely important to the Egyptians," Alice answered. "The Nile River was their lifeblood."

Reread the excerpt. **Underline** text evidence in paragraph 1 that shows Alice, a scientist, making an informed guess to answer a question she has.

COLLABORATE

Talk with a partner about how the author uses dialogue between Scott and Alice to tell facts about the ancient Egyptians.

What facts about ancient Egypt does the reader learn through the dialogue between the two characters?

_____

_____

_____

_____

Draw a box around text evidence that helped you find your answer.

Why does the author use factual details in this fictional mystery?

Talk About It Reread the excerpts on page 148-149. Talk with a partner about how the facts add to the mystery.

Cite Text Evidence What facts did the author include? What is the effect of the facts on the story? Write text evidence and your ideas in the chart.

Fact	Effect

Synthesize Information

Think about the way the author of the mystery conveys facts about ancient Egyptian history. How does this choice help readers learn more about the story's main character?

Write The author uses factual details in a fictional mystery because

_____

_____

_____

Point of View

Point of view is the narrator's perspective in a story. If the narrator is one of the story's characters, the story is told from first-person point of view. If the narrator is not a character, the point of view is third-person. A third-person limited narrator knows the thoughts and feelings of only one character. A third-person omniscient, or all-knowing, narrator knows the thoughts and feelings of every character.

 FIND TEXT EVIDENCE

In paragraph 2 on page 149, the first-person pronoun *I* describes the narrator's actions. This indicates the story is told from the first-person point of view.

> "Why were there so many boats found in the tomb?" <u>I wondered aloud.</u>
> "Wasn't Tutankhamun buried in the desert?"

 Your Turn Reread paragraphs 1–3 on page 149.

- How do readers learn the narrator's name? _____

  _____

- Why do you think the author chose to tell the mystery from a first-person point of view? _____

  _____

  _____

While first-person and third-person limited narrators may only know the thoughts and feelings of one character, they can provide observations of another character's appearance or actions. These observations can communicate to the reader what other characters may think or feel.

Text Connections

? **How does the photographer's documentation of this mummy compare with the author's description of the boat in *Pharaoh's Boat*?**

COLLABORATE

Talk About It Look at the photograph and read the caption. Talk with a partner about what you see. Discuss the value of having photographs of historical artifacts.

Cite Text Evidence **Circle** details in the photograph that tell about the ancient civilization this mummy was part of when he was alive. Think about how this artifact and the remains of the pharaoh's boat help scientists learn about other people and how they lived.

Write The photographer's work is like the

author's work because _____

_____

_____

_____

_____

_____

Quick Tip

Remember that artifacts are an important record of how people in a particular place and time lived. To compare the photographer's work to that of the author of *Pharaoh's Boat*, think about what details in the photograph tell you about the young man's culture.

This mummy was discovered and photographed so that scientists and archaeologists could learn about how the young man lived.

Present Your Work

COLLABORATE

Discuss how you will present your book about petroglyphs. Use the Presenting Checklist as you practice your presentation. Discuss the sentence starters below and write your answers.

Tech Tip

Consider using presentation software to share your book with your classmates. Make one slide for each page of your book.

✔ **Presenting Checklist**

☐ Assign speaking roles within your group. Make sure everyone has a role.

☐ Make sure your visuals can be clearly seen by everyone in your audience.

☐ Make eye contact with your audience.

☐ Speak at an appropriate rate and use a tone that is suited for an informational presentation.

In my research about petroglyphs, I realized _____

_____

_____

Now I would like to know more about _____

_____

_____

muha/123RF

Talk About It

The students in the photograph have been working all day getting ready for an art fair at school. They have more work to do at home on their art projects, but they wanted to take a break and relax a bit first. They decided to take a breather down by the playing field. They are enjoying being able to watch the sunset for a few minutes of recreation.

Look at the photograph. Talk to a partner about what you see and what you know about taking breaks. Why do you think the students chose this place to take a break? Where do you like to go to relax and take a break? Why do you think it is important to take breaks and relax for a while? Write your ideas about relaxing and why it is important in the web.

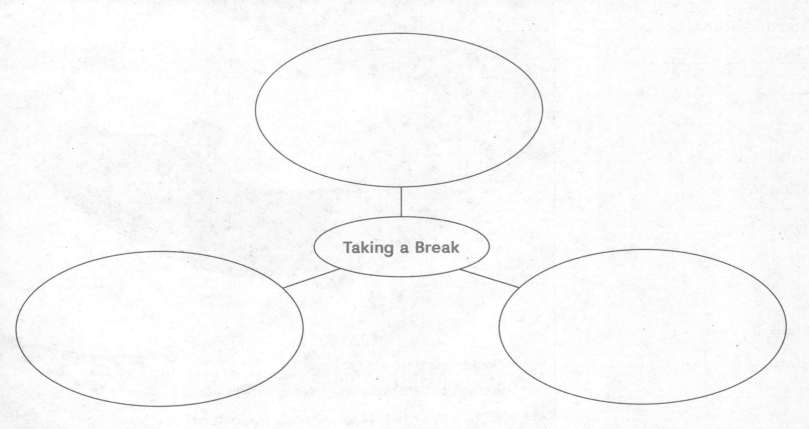

Taking a Break

Go online to **my.mheducation.com** and read the "Spare Time" Blast. Think about ways people like to spend their free time. What sorts of activities help people relax? Then blast back your response.

TAKE NOTES

Preview the poems by looking at the illustrations and reading the titles. Predict what you think each poem will be about. Write your prediction below. Then as you read, look for details that either confirm your prediction or help you revise it. Write your predictions below.

_____

_____

_____

As you read, take note of

Interesting Words _____

_____

_____

_____

Key Details _____

_____

_____

_____

_____

How Many Seconds?

Essential Question

? **Why is taking a break important?**

Read how two poets view opportunities for rest and renewal.

How many seconds in a minute?
Sixty, and no more in it.

How many minutes in an hour?
Sixty for sun and shower.

How many hours in a day?
Twenty-four for work and play.

How many days in a week?
Seven both to hear and speak.

How many weeks in a month?
Four, as the swift moon runn'th.

How many months in a year?
Twelve the almanack makes clear.

How many years in an age?
One hundred says the sage.

How many ages in time?
No one knows the rhyme.

—Christina Rossetti

FIND TEXT EVIDENCE

Read

Page 157

Repetition

Underline the words that repeat at the beginning of each stanza. What is the effect of repeating this phrase?

_____

_____

_____

Theme

Circle the response to the final question the speaker asks. How is this response different from the others in the poem?

_____

_____

_____

Reread

Author's Craft

How does the poet organize the order of the stanzas? Why do you think it is organized this way?

FIND TEXT EVIDENCE

Read

Page 158

Lyric Poetry and Ode

In an ode, a speaker praises something he or she admires. **Draw a box** around what the speaker is praising. **Circle** three words in the first stanza that show what the speaker is praising about this thing.

Theme

Underline details about the actions of the wind in the second stanza. What do they tell you about the speaker's feelings about the wind?

_____

_____

_____

_____

Reread

Author's Craft

How does the poet's use of sensory language in stanza 2 help you visualize the power of the wind?

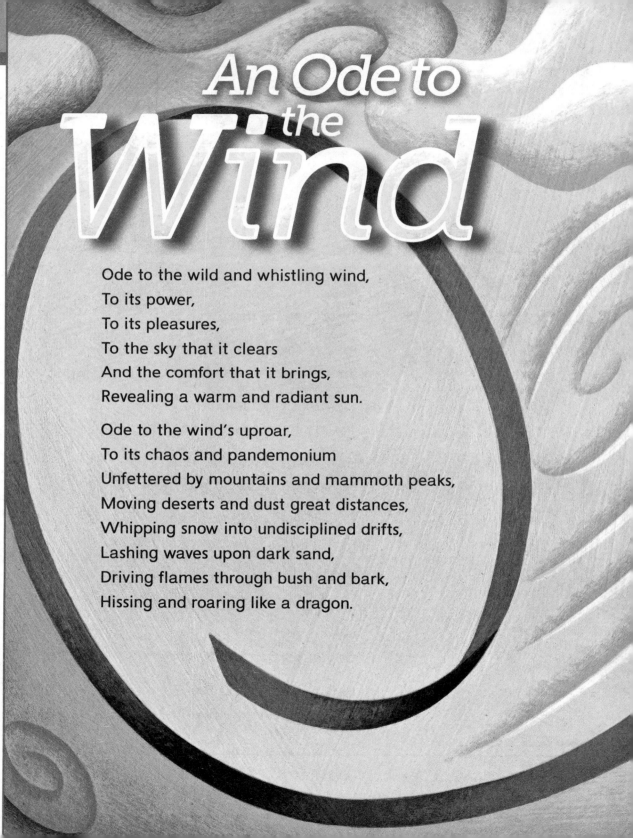

An Ode to the Wind

Ode to the wild and whistling wind,
To its power,
To its pleasures,
To the sky that it clears
And the comfort that it brings,
Revealing a warm and radiant sun.

Ode to the wind's uproar,
To its chaos and pandemonium
Unfettered by mountains and mammoth peaks,
Moving deserts and dust great distances,
Whipping snow into undisciplined drifts,
Lashing waves upon dark sand,
Driving flames through bush and bark,
Hissing and roaring like a dragon.

Ode to the wind's energy and titanic strength,
Scattering seeds as valuable as gold upon the land,
Filling square-rigged sails with billowing force,
Thrusting ships toward new horizons,
Whipping windmills to turn and generate,
Dispersing autumn leaves to replenish the earth,
To the storms it brings upon us
And the life-giving rain.

Ode to the moving air,
To the warm air rising
And the cool air that comes in to take its place,
To the sky that it cleared
And the comfort it brought,
Rustling hair, cooling fevered brows.
Wind a thousand times softer than silk
Offering a sweet incentive for recreation,
Lifting kites to the outer edge of the stratosphere.

—Jonathan Moss

Make Connections

How might experiencing the sensations of a windy day help you when you feel the need to take a break? Talk about whether your predictions on page 156 were confirmed.

FIND TEXT EVIDENCE

Read

Page 159

Imagery

Underline words and phrases that help readers both "see" and "feel" the wind's strength.

Hyperbole

Kites cannot really fly to the outer edge of the stratosphere. Why might the poet have used this exaggeration?

_____

_____

Reread

Author's Craft

Reread the last three lines. Why does the poet end with these details?

Fluency

Take turns with a partner reading the last stanza of "An Ode to the Wind." Discuss how you adjusted your expression and phrasing.

Vocabulary

Use the example sentences to talk with a partner about each word. Then answer the questions.

horizons

Living in many different areas of the country has helped me broaden my **horizons**.

How could you expand your horizons?

_____

_____

incentive

Ray offered his dog treats as an **incentive** to do tricks.

What incentive has convinced you to do something?

_____

_____

recreation

For **recreation**, Carla and Mina like to play basketball.

What do you like to do for recreation?

_____

_____

unfettered

The artist's **unfettered** creativity led her to make imaginative new forms of art.

What is a synonym for *unfettered*?

_____

_____

Poetry Terms

ode

I wrote an **ode** dedicated to my favorite fruit.

How can a poet express admiration for something in an ode?

_____

_____

imagery

A poem's **imagery** is developed through the use of sensory words and figurative language.

What does strong imagery in a poem help the reader understand?

_____

_____

repetition

A poet who uses **repetition** uses the same sounds, words, and phrases multiple times in a poem.

How can repetition affect the sound of a poem?

_____

_____

hyperbole

A poet uses **hyperbole** when the speaker makes an exaggerated claim about something.

How does hyperbole add to a description?

_____

_____

Build Your Word List Choose an unfamiliar word from one of the poems. Look up the word's meaning and origin, or the language it comes from, in a print or online dictionary. Write the word, its meaning, and its origin in your writer's notebook.

Figurative Language

Poets may emphasize a point by using **hyperbole**, which is an exaggeration that is not meant to be taken literally. The phrase *hotter than a million suns* is an example of hyperbole.

FIND TEXT EVIDENCE

When I read the line Wind a thousand times softer than silk, *I realize that the poet who wrote "An Ode to the Wind" is exaggerating to emphasize how soft wind can be. We can't actually feel something a thousand times softer than silk.*

Wind a thousand times softer than silk
Offering a sweet incentive for recreation,
Lifting kites to the outer edge of the stratosphere.

Your Turn Reread "An Ode to the Wind." Use hyperbole to either write a new line about wind or to add to an existing line in the poem.

_____

_____

Repetition and Imagery

Poets repeat words and phrases for emphasis. Repetition also affects how a poem sounds. Poets use imagery to paint a picture in the reader's mind. Imagery is often created through the use of sensory language.

🔍 FIND TEXT EVIDENCE

Reread "An Ode to the Wind" on pages 158–159. Identify repeated words and phrases. Then look for imagery created with vivid sensory language.

Page 158

Ode to the wind's uproar,
To its chaos and pandemonium
Unfettered by mountains and mammoth peaks,
Moving deserts and dust great distances,
Whipping snow into undisciplined drifts,
Lashing waves upon dark sand,
Driving flames through bush and bark,
Hissing and roaring like a dragon.

Each stanza of the poem begins with the words "Ode to" and tells about a different aspect of the wind. In this stanza, the poet uses images of snow, waves, and fire to help the reader "feel" the wind's fearful strength.

Your Turn Find another example of repetition and imagery in "An Ode to the Wind." What ideas do they emphasize?

_____

_____

_____

_____

Lyric Poetry and Ode

Lyric poetry expresses the speaker's thoughts and feelings. It often has a musical quality and doesn't always rhyme. An **ode** is a type of lyric poem. Odes praise a person, natural occurrence, object, or concept.

 FIND TEXT EVIDENCE

I can tell that "An Ode to the Wind" is an ode because of its title and because the speaker praises different qualities of the wind. It is also a lyric poem because it expresses the speaker's feelings.

Word Wise

An ode usually contains three or more stanzas. The stanzas often reflect a pattern or structure. For example, the second and third stanzas in "An Ode to the Wind" have the same number of lines.

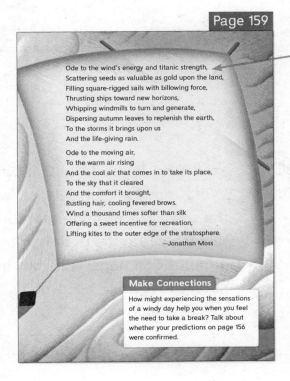

Page 159

Ode to the wind's energy and titanic strength,
Scattering seeds as valuable as gold upon the land,
Filling square-rigged sails with billowing force,
Thrusting ships toward new horizons,
Whipping windmills to turn and generate,
Dispersing autumn leaves to replenish the earth,
To the storms it brings upon us
And the life-giving rain.

Ode to the moving air,
To the warm air rising
And the cool air that comes in to take its place,
To the sky that it cleared
And the comfort it brought,
Rustling hair, cooling fevered brows.
Wind a thousand times softer than silk
Offering a sweet incentive for recreation,
Lifting kites to the outer edge of the stratosphere.
—Jonathan Moss

Make Connections

How might experiencing the sensations of a windy day help you when you feel the need to take a break? Talk about whether your predictions on page 156 were confirmed.

This ode praises the wind, which is a natural occurrence. The choice of words shows the speaker's feelings about the subject.

 COLLABORATE **Your Turn** Reread "How Many Seconds?" on pages 156–157. Is it a lyric poem? Is it an ode? Explain your reasons.

_____

_____

_____

_____

_____

Theme

A poem's **theme** is its overall idea, or message, about life. To determine the theme, look for clues that show how the speaker feels about the topic.

🔍 FIND TEXT EVIDENCE

When I reread "How Many Seconds?" I'll pay attention to details that reveal the speaker's attitude toward the subject. Thinking about all the details together helps me identify the poem's theme.

Detail
In each stanza, the speaker lists a unit of time. The units are ordered from smallest to largest.

↓

Detail
The speaker describes how each unit of time is commonly measured and lived.

↓

Detail
In the last stanza, readers learn there is no "rhyme," or way to measure the number of ages in time.

↓

Theme
Time is something that can be measured yet is also infinite.

Your Turn Reread "An Ode to the Wind" and look for details that convey the speaker's attitude toward the subject. Write the details in the graphic organizer on page 165. Then use the details to identify a theme in "An Ode to the Wind."

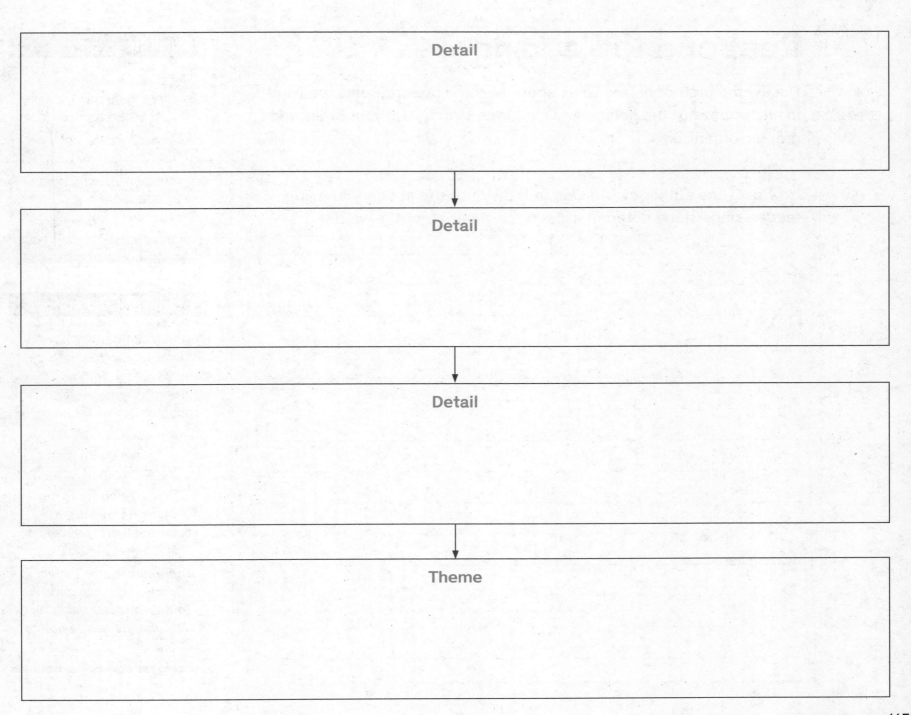

Detail

Detail

Detail

Theme

Respond to Reading

COLLABORATE

Discuss the prompt below. Think about how the poet presents the wind in each stanza of the poem "An Ode to the Wind." Use your notes and graphic organizer.

How does the author of "An Ode to the Wind" use imagery to help readers understand different aspects, or qualities, of the wind?

_____

_____

_____

_____

_____

_____

_____

_____

_____

_____

_____

_____

_____

_____

_____

Quick Tip

Use these sentence starters to discuss the text and to organize ideas.

- *In each stanza, the poet uses imagery to . . .*
- *The phrase . . . appeals to the sense of . . .*
- *The speaker describes the wind as . . .*

Grammar Connections

When citing text evidence in a response to poetry, make sure to follow proper grammar and punctuation conventions.

- Put quotation marks around a direct quote from the poem.
- When referring to more than one line, use a slash mark to indicate a line break.

The speaker uses the lines "Ode to the moving air, / To the warm air rising" to describe the gentle nature of the wind.

Collect Data

When you **collect data**, you gather information about a topic that you will measure and analyze. For some topics, researchers conduct surveys to collect relevant data. For example, for a pet study, researchers may want to know how many people in a neighborhood have a pet and, if so, what type of pet they have. Respondents answer specific questions, and their responses are recorded and analyzed by researchers.

Why is it importance to not influence how respondents answer the questions?

_____

_____

_____

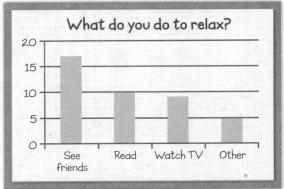

What do you do to relax?

Create a Bar Graph With a partner, conduct a survey to determine where people you know prefer to take a break, and then create a bar graph that displays the results. Use the following tips to conduct your survey and collect data:

- Come up with a list of 5–6 answer possibilities, such as "in my room," "in my backyard," "at my friend's house," and so on.
- Survey respondents both in and out of school.
- Avoid favoring any particular answer. Simply read respondents the question and ask them to choose a response.

Discuss how you will display your bar graph and conclusions. Also, talk about how additional visuals or even audio might engage your audience. You will present your bar graph to your class.

A student created this bar graph to show the results of a survey about how people relax.

- The title of the graph shows the question that respondents were asked to answer.
- The *x*-axis runs horizontally and shows the answer choices.
- The *y*-axis runs vertically and shows the number of responses.
- The bars show how many people chose each response.

To You

 How does the imagery in the poem connect to the poem's theme?

Literature Anthology: pages 464–466

Talk About It Reread **Literature Anthology** page 465. Talk with a partner about the examples of imagery in "To You."

Cite Text Evidence What words and phrases contribute to the theme of the poem?

Clue

↓

Clue

↓

Clue

↓

Theme

Write The imagery connects to the theme by _____

_____

_____

Make Inferences

Think about what the speaker is asking "you" to do. You can use the speaker's request to help yourself better understand the poem's theme.

Ode to Pablo's Tennis Shoes

 How does the speaker use Pablo's shoes to convey the theme of this poem?

 Talk About It Reread the poem on **Literature Anthology** page 466. Talk with a partner about how the speaker describes the tennis shoes.

Cite Text Evidence What words and phrases describe the tennis shoes? Write text evidence in the web and tell the poem's theme.

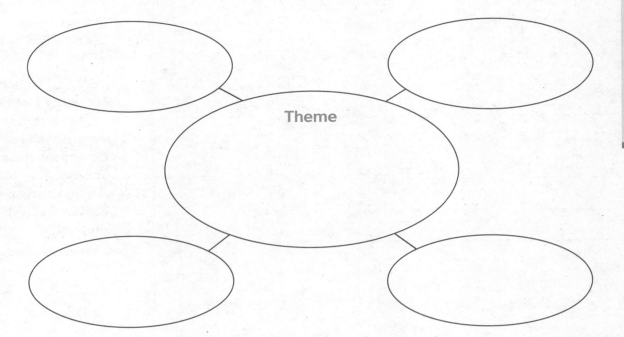

Theme

 Make Inferences

In the third stanza, the speaker says that Pablo "wants to be / Like his shoes." Use details about the shoes and about Pablo to explain why that is.

Quick Tip

There can be more than one theme in a poem. There are no wrong answers about theme, as long as you have accurate text evidence to support your ideas.

Write The speaker uses Pablo's shoes to convey theme by _____

_____

_____

Respond to Reading

COLLABORATE

Discuss the prompt below. Apply your own knowledge of how poets use imagery to convey important messages to readers. Use your notes and graphic organizer.

Compare how each poet shares his common message of the importance of taking a break.

_____

_____

_____

_____

_____

_____

_____

_____

_____

_____

_____

_____

_____

_____

Drumbeat
Sittin' on the Dock of the Bay

*Literature Anthology:
pages 468–469*

? **How does the poet use sensory language to create the urban and natural imagery in the poem "Drumbeat"?**

Talk About It Reread the poem "Drumbeat" on **Literature Anthology** page 468. Talk with a partner about what each stanza describes.

Cite Text Evidence What sensory language is used to create the urban imagery and the natural imagery? Write text evidence in the chart.

As you read, pause to visualize each image. Which sense is being appealed to? Do some images appeal to more than one sense?

Quick Tip

As you read, pause to visualize each image. Which sense is being appealed to? Do some images appeal to more than one sense?

Urban Imagery	Natural Imagery

Write The poet creates urban and natural imagery by using sensory language that _____

_____

_____

_____

Reread | PAIRED SELECTION

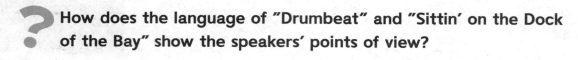 **How does the language of "Drumbeat" and "Sittin' on the Dock of the Bay" show the speakers' points of view?**

Talk About It Reread "Drumbeat" and "Sittin' on the Dock of the Bay" on **Literature Anthology** pages 468–469. With a partner, determine the point of view of each poem.

Cite Text Evidence What phrases help you figure out each point of view? Write text evidence and explain.

Point of View	Text Evidence

Write The words and phrases the poets use convey two distinct points of view that say _____

_____

_____

Mood

Mood is the atmosphere and emotion created in a piece of writing. **Imagery** can help a poet convey a mood by creating mental images in a reader's mind. A poet carefully chooses words and phrases to create a certain atmosphere and evoke feelings in the readers.

FIND TEXT EVIDENCE

Reread "Sittin' on the Dock of the Bay" on **Literature Anthology** page 469 aloud. The image of someone sitting all day in the sun on a dock, watching ships come in and out, creates a relaxed, peaceful mood.

Your Turn Reread "Drumbeat" on page 468.

- How would you describe the mood in the first stanza? Explain your answer. Include how imagery adds to the mood. _____

  _____

  _____

  _____

  _____

- Does the mood change or stay the same in the second stanza? _____

  _____

  _____

  _____

  _____

Text Connections

? How do the songwriters who wrote "Sittin' on the Dock of the Bay" and "I Don't Care if the Rain Comes Down" and the poet who wrote "To You" share their speakers' points of view?

Talk About It Read the song lyrics. Talk with a partner about what the song means. Discuss why the writer uses repetition.

Cite Text Evidence **Underline** how the speaker feels about dancing.

Write I know how the speakers in the song and poems

feel because _____

_____

_____

_____

_____

_____

_____

_____

> **Quick Tip**
>
> To better understand why repetition is used in "I Don't Care if the Rain Comes Down," think about what the repeated words and phrases might mean to the speaker.

I Don't Care if the Rain Comes Down

American Folk Song

I don't care if the rain comes down,
I'm gonna dance all day,
I don't care if the rain comes down,
I'm gonna dance all day.

Hey, hey, carry me away,
I'm gonna dance all day,
Hey, hey, carry me away,
I'm gonna dance all day.

Expression and Phrasing

When you read a poem aloud, think about the emotion the speaker is showing. This will help you identify the **expression** needed to convey his or her thoughts and feelings. Paying attention to **phrasing**, or when to pause while reading, can also convey a poem's meaning. Consider how certain words are grouped together when spoken aloud. Commas, periods, and other punctuation marks can also indicate phrasing.

Quick Tip

Preview a poem before reading it aloud to understand its overall meaning, as well as the meaning of all the words. Make sure your expression matches the meaning of the words in each part of the poem.

Page 158

Ode to the wild and whistling wind,

To its power,

To its pleasures,

To the sky that it clears

And the comfort that it brings,

Revealing a warm and radiant sun.

Notice that this stanza is actually one long sentence. The commas at the ends of the first, second, third, and fifth lines break up the sentence and indicate when to pause between phrases.

Your Turn Take turns reading aloud with a partner the second stanza of "An Ode to the Wind" on page 158. Visualize the feelings the speaker describes, and express these feelings as you read. Use punctuation to guide phrasing.

Afterward, think about how you did. Complete these sentences.

I remembered to _____

_____

Next time, I will _____

_____

WRITING

Expert Model

*Literature Anthology:
pages 464–466*

Features of an Ode

An ode is a type of lyric poem. It is written to praise a person, natural occurrence, object, or idea. It often has three or more stanzas that reflect a pattern or structure. An ode

- expresses thoughts and emotions;

- often has sound devices, such as rhyme and repetition, that create a musical quality and emphasize important ideas;

- often uses sensory and figurative language.

Word Wise

Sensory language appeals to the five senses. This helps readers create a mental image while they read, complete with sounds, sights, feelings, and sometimes even smells and tastes. Read the last five lines of "Ode to Pablo's Tennis Shoes." Think about what this imagery tells you about Pablo and his shoes.

Analyze an Expert Model Studying odes will help you learn how to plan and write an ode of your own. **Reread** "Ode to Pablo's Tennis Shoes" on **Literature Anthology** page 466. Write your answers to the questions below.

How do you know Pablo's specific feelings about his sneakers? _____

_____

_____

_____

What is an effect of the repetition of the words "his shoes" in the poem?

_____

_____

_____

Plan: Choose Your Topic

COLLABORATE

Freewrite Think about what you like to do to relax or take a break. Why do you choose to do this? What images come to mind when you think about what you like to do? How does taking a break make you feel? Quickly write your ideas on the lines below without stopping. Then discuss your ideas with a partner.

Quick Tip

Ideas for the topic of your ode may include reading a book, hanging out with friends, playing a game, listening to music, doing something physical, or spending time outside.

_____

_____

_____

_____

_____

Writing Prompt Use the ideas from your freewriting to write an ode to what you do to relax or take a break.

I will write an ode to _____

Purpose and Audience Think about who will read or hear your poem. Will your purpose be to inform, persuade, or entertain this audience? How will you help the reader understand the speaker's feelings?

Plan In your writer's notebook, make a Topic and Details organizer to plan the details you will include in your poem. Put your topic in the center and fill in at least three details.

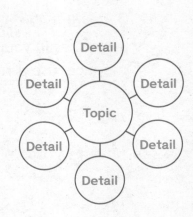

Plan: Sound Devices

Repetition of Words and Sounds Sound devices, such as rhyme and repetition, create a musical quality and can add meaning to an ode. While odes don't have to rhyme, they may feature rhyming for effect. Repeated words and phrases can emphasize important ideas in the poem.

As you plan sound devices for your poem, consider these questions:

- Do I want to use rhyme in my poem?

- What words and phrases do I want to repeat to emphasize important ideas in my poem?

List important words you may want to repeat or rhyme within your poem.

_____

_____

_____

_____

 Graphic Organizer Once you have determined how you will use sound devices in your poem, fill in the rest of your organizer. If you need more space, use a separate sheet of paper in your writer's notebook.

Word Wise

Remember that rhyme can be used in many ways. Even just rhyming a couple of words in the same line can emphasize meaning and affect the sound of a poem.

Here are some other sound devices you might want to use in your poem:

- **Alliteration:** the use of words with the same beginning consonant sounds, as in *bye-bye, beautiful bird!*

- **Onomatopoeia:** the use of a word whose sound suggests its meaning, such as *purr, crackle,* and *swoosh.*

Draft

Sensory Language Poets use sensory language, or language that appeals to the five senses, to help readers visualize and "experience" what is happening. As you read the example below from "An Ode to the Wind," pay attention to details that appeal to your senses of hearing and touch.

Quick Tip

When choosing sensory language, think about the effect you are trying to achieve. What do you want the reader to understand and experience? What vivid adjectives and verbs will best express your ideas?

> Ode to the wild and whistling wind,
> To its power,
> To its pleasures,
> To the sky that it clears
> And the comfort that it brings,
> Revealing a warm and radiant sun.

Now use the above excerpt as a model to incorporate sensory language into a few lines that could go in your own poem.

_____

_____

_____

_____

_____

Write a Draft Use your graphic organizer to help you write your draft in your writer's notebook. Use sensory language to help readers visualize what is happening and to convey the details of your speaker's thoughts and feelings. Consider where to include sound devices.

Revise

Figurative Language Poets often use figurative language to create images and deepen readers' understanding of the text. Figurative language includes metaphor, simile, personification, and hyperbole. Read the lines below. Then revise them by adding figurative language.

> The backyard has
>
> Soft grass to lie on
>
> Where I can let my mind wander
>
> Under the gentle rustle of leaves.

_____

_____

_____

_____

 Revision Revise your draft. Identify places where you can make meaningful comparisons or incorporate other figurative language.

John Lund/Sam Diephuis/Blend Images/age fotostock

Word Wise

Similes are comparisons that use the words _like_ or _as_: _The night sky was like a blanket of stars._

Metaphors are indirect comparisons without _like_ or _as_: _The night sky was a blanket of stars._

Personification describes objects and animals as if they were human: _The flowers waved hello in the wind._

Hyperbole is an exaggeration not meant to be taken literally: _I'm so hungry I could eat an entire orchard of apples._

Peer Conferences

Review a Draft Listen carefully as a partner reads his or her work aloud. Take notes about what you liked and what was difficult to follow. Begin by telling what you liked about the draft. Ask questions that will help the writer think more about the writing. Make suggestions that you think will make the writing stronger. Use these sentence starters.

I enjoyed this part of your draft because . . .

I have a question about . . .

This part is unclear to me. Can you explain why . . . ?

More sensory language would help me visualize . . .

Partner Feedback After your partner gives you feedback on your draft, write one of the suggestions that you will use in your revision. Refer to the rubric on page 183 as you give feedback.

Based on my partner's feedback, I will _____

_____

_____

After you finish giving each other feedback, reflect on the peer conference. What was helpful? What might you do differently next time?

Revision As you revise your draft, use the Revising Checklist to help you figure out what text you may need to move, elaborate on, or delete. Remember to use the rubric on page 183 to help you with your revision.

✔ Revising Checklist

- ☐ Is it clear what is being praised and why?
- ☐ Have I used sound devices effectively to create a musical effect and/or emphasize ideas?
- ☐ Did I use enough sensory language to help readers visualize what is happening?
- ☐ Have I used figurative language?

Edit and Proofread

When you **edit** and **proofread** your writing, you look for and correct mistakes in spelling, punctuation, capitalization, and grammar. Reading through a revised draft multiple times can help you make sure you're correcting any errors. Use the checklist below to edit your sentences.

✓ Editing Checklist

- ☐ Is there a space between each stanza in your poem?
- ☐ Are all pronouns in the proper case?
- ☐ Are irregular verbs used correctly?
- ☐ Is the first word of each line capitalized?
- ☐ Is punctuation used thoughtfully?
- ☐ Are all words spelled correctly?

Grammar Connections

Spelling and grammar checkers are not always effective when reviewing poetry because poems often don't follow the rules for grammar and usage. Proofread your poem carefully, word by word. Think about the purpose of any unconventional grammar and punctuation. These choices should add meaning to your poem; otherwise, they look like mistakes.

List two mistakes you found as you proofread your ode.

1 _____

_____

2 _____

_____

Publish, Present, and Evaluate

Publishing When you **publish** your writing, you create a clean, neat final copy that is free of mistakes. As you write, be sure your writing is legible.

Presentation When you are ready to **present** your work, rehearse your presentation. Use the Presenting Checklist to help you.

Evaluate After you publish your writing, use the rubric below to **evaluate** your writing.

What did you do successfully? _____

_____

What needs more work? _____

_____

4	3	2	1
• it is clear what the ode is praising and why it is being praised • effectively uses sound devices to create a clear musical quality or to emphasize ideas • includes both vivid and meaningful sensory and figurative language	• it is mostly clear what the ode is praising and why it is being praised • uses sound devices to create a musical quality or to emphasize ideas • includes some sensory language and figurative language	• it is not clear either what the ode is praising or why it is being praised • uses sound devices inconsistently for uneven musical quality or emphasis • includes very little sensory language and figurative language	• nothing is praised, or it is unclear why something is being praised • does not use sound devices; poem lacks any musical quality or emphasis • uses no sensory language or figurative language

Spiral Review

You have learned new skills and strategies in Unit 6 that will help you read more critically. Now it is time to practice what you have learned.

- **Make Inferences**
- **Photographs**
- **Main Idea and Key Details**
- **Figurative Language**
- **Theme**
- **Latin Roots**
- **Greek Roots**
- **Imagery**

Connect to Content

- **Compare and Contrast Chart**
- **"World Wonders in Danger"**

Read the selection and choose the best answer to each question.

5,000 YEARS OF PRINTING

[1] Today, printing is easy and efficient. Industrial printers can print thousands of books, magazines, or newspapers in a short amount of time. Individuals can print almost anything they desire from a personal or library printer. But printing was not always quite so effortless. Modern printing is the product of thousands of years of technological innovation and progress.

Ancient scrolls (top) made from papyrus (bottom) have helped us learn about Egypt's past.

EARLY WRITING ON PAPYRUS

[2] Thousands of years ago, a reedy plant called *papyrus* grew in abundance along the Nile River. Ancient Egyptians used this natural resource in many ways. They wove the reeds into baskets and rope, bundled the sturdy part of the stalks to build ships, and ate the softer part of the stalks as food.

[3] But papyrus may be most significant because it was used to create a material similar to paper. In fact, the word *paper* comes from *papyrus*. We know how paper from papyrus was made and used because art preserved in the tombs of pharaohs shows the process. After the papyrus plant was cut, it was harvested, beaten flat, and rolled into scrolls.

[4] The process of making scrolls required a lot of work, so papyrus scrolls were expensive and usually available only to trained scribes. Boys training to be <u>scribes</u> practiced writing on other materials, such as wooden boards or slabs of clay. Once a student had finished his training, he would receive a papyrus scroll, pens and brushes made from thin reeds, and black and red inks made from minerals, such as iron oxide or coal. Some ancient papyrus scrolls still exist and have helped us learn more about early writing systems.

WOODBLOCK PRINTING

Each carved woodblock could be used to print one Chinese character.

5   Papyrus scrolls were useful as writing surfaces, but there wasn't a way to make a copy of a text without rewriting it by hand. Around the fourth century, the Chinese began to use woodblocks like a stamp to make multiple copies of one text. Craftsmen would carve a design into a woodblock, rub dye on the block, and press the block on silk cloth. This wasn't just writing; it was printing.

6   But like papyrus scrolls, silk was expensive. By the seventh century, the Chinese had begun making paper from the bark of the mulberry tree. This stronger, less expensive resource made it easier for Chinese printers to create larger amounts of printed material.

7   Printing improved further in the eleventh century with the innovative ideas of a man named Bi Sheng. Bi Sheng had the idea to carve individual characters into pieces of clay. He would then apply an ink made from ashes, wax, and pine tree resin. Finally, he would press the inked clay on a writing surface. The process was like woodblock printing, but because each clay form had its own character carved into it, Bi Sheng could move the pieces around and reuse each block to make a greater variety of prints. This was the start of what is known today as *movable type*.

GUTENBERG'S PRINTING PRESS

These individual letters on metal type can be rearranged to form a variety of words.

8   Another significant advancement in printing happened in the fifteenth century. A German man named Johannes Gutenberg invented a machine called a printing press. Gutenberg formed individual letters on separate pieces of metal. He could fit the pieces tightly together to form whole words, which could then be used to build sentences and paragraphs. After adding ink to the pieces, he could print whole pages to be bound into books. After a book was printed, the individual pieces could be reused for other projects. Gutenberg's printing press made it possible to print many copies of the same book in a short time.

PRINTING TODAY

9   Since Gutenberg's time, printing methods have continued to improve. Today's printing presses can print up to 300 pages per minute. Thanks to brilliant advances in printing technology over thousands of years, it is easier than ever to provide books and other written materials to readers throughout the world.

1 The Latin root *scrib* means "write." In paragraph 4, <u>scribes</u> were people who —

   A wrote Egyptian laws

   B read written texts aloud

   C delivered handwritten letters

   D wrote text on papyrus scrolls

2 What can readers infer after reading paragraph 8?

   F Gutenberg's printing press made printing faster.

   G Few texts were printed in Europe before the fifteenth century.

   H Ink was in limited supply in Gutenberg's time.

   J Gutenberg's printing press was very easy to build.

3 The photographs and captions on page 185 help readers understand that metal type —

   A requires more training to use than woodblocks

   B costs more to operate than woodblocks

   C gives printers more flexibility than woodblocks

   D produces higher-quality printed materials than woodblocks

4 What is the main idea of the selection?

   F People have always wanted to record their ideas on paper.

   G Modern printing is the result of many technological innovations.

   H Computers have made it easier to print than ever before in history.

   J The Chinese invention of movable type was extremely important.

> **Quick Tip**
>
> Sometimes you must infer in order to answer a question. Before responding, scan the text again to identify evidence that supports your inference.

Read the selection and choose the best answer to each question.

From Up Here

The peak of a mountain
Reaches high
Into the deep blue sky
Of a summer morning.

5 A high and hot and brilliant Sun
Casts its light through
The cold and dark of the <u>cosmos</u>
To brighten the world.

Breathe deeply.
10 Sweat has darkened clothing.
Rest against a slim pine
And look out across the landscape.

Great rolling hills,
Green and hazy in the distance,
15 And winding streams
Remind one of a painting.

Plots of farmland
Like patches on a quilt
As if this great quilt
20 Were thrown over Earth itself.

A cooling breeze
Whispers through a forest
Of old crooked trees
That has been here forever.

25 Enjoy this short rest
Among old pines and older rocks
After a long climb
Up a steep and stubborn trail.

A small bird sits in a tree.
30 Even a robin needs a rest,
For building a nest
Must be hard work.

Why hike
If not to enjoy the view?
35 Why build a nest
If not for a place to sleep?

Work is important
But rest no less so.
This the robin knows.
40 Do you?

1 The Greek root *cosm* means "universe." What does <u>cosmos</u> mean in line 7?

A Earth

B outer space

C air

D daytime

Quick Tip

If two answers seem correct, compare them to identify how they are different. This can make it easier to find the correct answer.

2 Which of the following lines from the poem contains imagery?

F A high and hot and brilliant Sun

G Remind one of a painting

H After a long climb

J This the robin knows.

3 Which of the following lines from the poem contains hyperbole?

A Rest against a slim pine

B That has been here forever.

C Among old pines and older rocks

D Up a steep and stubborn trail.

4 Which of the following best describes the main theme of the poem?

F Rest is just as important as work.

G Birds are hard workers.

H Hiking a mountain is challenging.

J If an activity becomes too hard, you should quit.

EXTEND YOUR LEARNING

COMPARING GENRES

Reread the lyric poem "To You" on **Literature Anthology** page 465 and the mystery "The Mystery of the Missing Sandals" on pages 460–463. Then use the Venn diagram to compare and contrast the two selections. Think about genre characteristics to identify the similarities and differences.

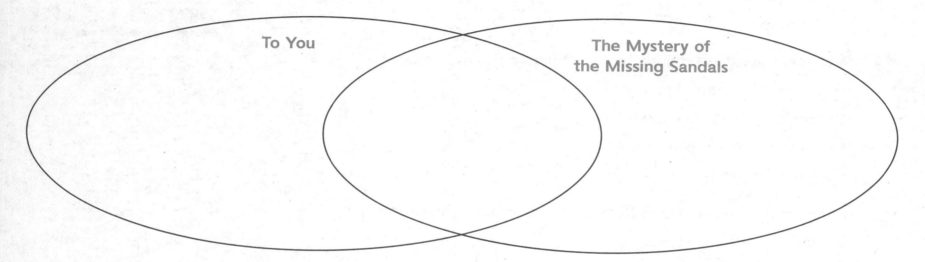

To You

The Mystery of the Missing Sandals

FIGURATIVE LANGUAGE

Figurative language allows writers to create a mental image in a reader's mind. An author might use a metaphor or simile to make an interesting comparison. A fiction writer or poet may use personification to help readers understand or relate to an idea, or hyperbole to emphasize a point.

- On the lines below, record one interesting use of figurative language from one of the selections. Record additional examples in your writer's notebook.

_____

_____

ANALYZE PLOT

Plot is the sequence of events in a story. After the introduction, **rising action** builds on the conflict, or problem, characters face. The action leads to the **climax**, or turning point, of the story. **Falling action** refers to events that lead to the **resolution** when the conflict is resolved and the story ends.

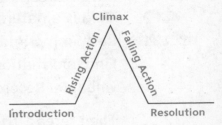

- Reread "The Mystery of the Missing Sandals" on **Literature Anthology** pages 460–463. Analyze the plot by identifying plot events that make up the rising action, climax, falling action, and resolution.

Rising Action: _____

Climax: _____

Falling Action: _____

Resolution: _____

FLASHBACK

A **flashback** is a part of a story that interrupts the chronological order of events to tell about an event that happened at an earlier time. An author may use a flashback to give readers background information that is important to understanding a story's plot.

- Find and describe a flashback in "The Mystery of the Missing Sandals." Explain why the author includes the flashback in the story.

_____

_____

_____

_____

COMPARE AND CONTRAST CHART

COLLABORATE

Gold is a natural resource that people have valued throughout history. Research print and digital sources to learn more about gold and its history. Find information about where gold is found, how it is used, and why it is valuable. Record your answers in the chart below.

Then reread *The Story of Salt* on **Literature Anthology** pages 420–435 and complete the chart. If necessary, do research to find more facts about salt. With a partner, discuss how gold and salt are similar and different.

	Gold	Salt
Where It Is Found		
How It Is Used		
Why It Is Valuable		

WORLD WONDERS IN DANGER

SOCIAL STUDIES

Log on to **my.mheducation.com** and reread the *Time for Kids* online article "World Wonders in Danger," including the information found in the interactive elements. Then answer the questions below.

- What is the purpose of the World Monuments Watch list?

- Review the interactive map. In what part of the world are the largest number of the 2012 WMF sites located?

- Why are sites on the World Monuments Watch list endangered?

- Describe how the author presents the information about cultural-heritage sites. Why is this text organization effective?

World Wonders in Danger
A list identifies 67 endangered sites, both ancient and modern.

Time for Kids: "World Wonders in Danger"

TRACK YOUR PROGRESS

WHAT DID YOU LEARN?

Use the rubric to evaluate yourself on the skills you learned in this unit.
Write your scores in the boxes below.

4	3	2	1
I can successfully identify all examples of this skill.	I can identify most examples of this skill.	I can identify a few examples of this skill.	I need to work more on this skill.

☐ Main Idea and Key Details   ☐ Latin Roots   ☐ Theme

☐ Sequence   ☐ Greek Roots   ☐ Hyperbole

Something that I need to work more on is ＿＿＿＿＿＿＿＿＿ because

＿＿＿＿＿＿＿＿＿＿＿＿＿＿＿＿＿＿＿＿＿＿＿＿＿＿＿

＿＿＿＿＿＿＿＿＿＿＿＿＿＿＿＿＿＿＿＿＿＿＿＿＿＿＿

＿＿＿＿＿＿＿＿＿＿＿＿＿＿＿＿＿＿＿＿＿＿＿＿＿＿＿

Text to Self Think back over the texts that you have read in this unit.
Choose one text and write a short paragraph explaining a personal
connection that you have made to the text.

I made a personal connection to ＿＿＿＿＿＿ because ＿＿＿＿＿＿

＿＿＿＿＿＿＿＿＿＿＿＿＿＿＿＿＿＿＿＿＿＿＿＿＿＿＿

＿＿＿＿＿＿＿＿＿＿＿＿＿＿＿＿＿＿＿＿＿＿＿＿＿＿＿

＿＿＿＿＿＿＿＿＿＿＿＿＿＿＿＿＿＿＿＿＿＿＿＿＿＿＿

＿＿＿＿＿＿＿＿＿＿＿＿＿＿＿＿＿＿＿＿＿＿＿＿＿＿＿

Present Your Work

COLLABORATE

Discuss how you will present your bar graph displaying the data you collected on where people prefer to take a break. Use the Presenting Checklist as you practice your presentation. Discuss the sentence starters below and write your answers.

One discovery I made by surveying people about where they like to take breaks is _____

_____

_____

Now I would like to conduct a survey about _____

_____

_____

Monkey Business Images/Shutterstock